Jan Fook lectures in the Graduate School of Social Work at La Trobe University, Melbourne. She is the author of *Radical Casework*.

Studies in Society

Titles include:

Studies in Society

THE REFLECTIVE RESEARCHER

Social workers' theories of practice research

Edited by Jan Fook

ALLEN & UNWIN

1996

For Al

First published in 1996
Allen & Unwin Pty Ltd
9 Atchison Street, St Leonards, NSW 2065 Australia

National Library of Australia
Cataloguing-in-Publication data

The reflective researcher: social workers' experience with
  theories of practice research.

  Includes index.
  ISBN 1 86448 033 5.

  1. Social service—Research. 2. Social case work.
  I. Fook, Janis. (Series: Studies in society (Sydney, N.S.W.)).

361.32072

Set in 10/11 pt Sabon by DOCUPRO, Sydney
Printed by KHL Printing Company (Pte) Ltd, Singapore

10 9 8 7 6 5 4 3 2 1

Contents

Acknowledgments

Who can say where the ideas for a book come from?

Many of the ideas were sparked off through work and discussions with Bill Healy and Lindsay Napier. Bill introduced me to Argyris and Schon's *Theory in Practice*, and Schon's *Educating the Reflective Practitioner* which, among other things, inspired the title of this book. Many of my ideas were also triggered by, and have informed, research projects that I have been involved in with Linette Hawkins and Martin Ryan.

Thanks are due to all the contributors. They all made extra special efforts to take seriously my rigorous deadlines. In the face of other pressing demands, they have made a commendable effort to see this book through to completion.

Finally, Allan Kellehear has been in both unobtrusive and obtrusive ways the kind of friend, colleague and partner every academic would wish for. This book is dedicated to him.

Contributors

Helen Cleak is lecturer in social work at La Trobe University, Melbourne, Australia, teaching direct practice, field education, and health and social work. She has also worked concurrently at Box Hill Hospital, Melbourne, for several years and has been part of the management team there. She is actively involved in case-mix issues, represents social work on a number of state committees, and has recently completed doctoral research on discharge planning.

Robert Doyle is professor of social work and director of the Centre for Rural Social Research at Charles Sturt University, Wagga Wagga, Australia. He has alternated between practice and academic positions during his professional career, keeping a strong link between the two. He has researched and practised in the areas of community attitudes towards delinquency, community mental health, and use of neighbourhood community workers. He conducted a landmark study on access and equity within human services in Canada which subsequently led to research and consulting work in Australia.

Jan Fook has social work degrees from the universities of New South Wales and Sydney, and has taught in social work and welfare courses around Australia over the last fifteen years. She is currently senior lecturer in social work at La Trobe University. Her main research and teaching interests have been in social work practice, and she is probably best known for her book *Radical Casework: A Theory of Practice* (Allen & Unwin, 1993). She has also written about and researched feminist social work, rural social work, and more recently the development of social work expertise. With Bill Healy, she has been involved in teaching one of the first postgraduate advanced social work practice courses in Australia. In 1993 she wrote a new undergraduate social work course for Deakin University, Geelong, Australia. She has run a number of workshops on publishing for practitioners, and has most recently become involved in a new Australian Association of Social Workers special interest group for practice research in Melbourne.

Sue Gleed is lecturer and field education coordinator in the Bachelor of Social Work program at Northern Territory University, Darwin, Australia. She has worked as a social worker in both government and non-government organisations, and has lived and worked in northern Australia for the last twelve years. Her research interests include the non-government welfare sector, international social work and remote area social work.

Linette Hawkins is a social worker with graduate diplomas in applied sociology and public policy. She 'dropped in and out' of the public service for twenty years until she vowed never to return in the late 1980s. Since then she has been engaged in a diverse range of positions and research projects as a freelancer. During the last few years her principal employment has been in field education programs for community development, welfare and social work courses at Royal Melbourne Institute of Technology, and Deakin and La Trobe universities. She is a member of the Action Research Issues Association based in Melbourne.

Bill Healy is senior lecturer in social work at La Trobe University. He has extensive experience in practice and academic settings, and is well known for his work in the mental health field. 'My interest in practice research goes back to my student days, although we didn't call it "reflective analysis" then, not least because it occurred in the pubs and coffee lounges of Carlton!' he says. 'In more recent years I have pursued the nature of public welfare practice with a particular interest in the interplay of policy, politics, organisation processes and practice difficulties and opportunities. In both my research and teaching I seek to make better sense of the constantly changing dynamic of theory, practice, context and values that characterises the work world of social work.'

Gary Hough is senior lecturer in social work at Royal Melbourne Institute of Technology, where he coordinates the Master of Social Science (Community Services Management) program. He worked as a practitioner in public welfare for many years before moving into social work education. His teaching and research interests are in community services organisation and management, program planning and evaluation, and public welfare policy and practice. He holds a doctoral degree from La Trobe University.

Ann Ingamells lectures in community development and women's studies at Edith Cowan University in Perth, Australia. She has been involved in a wide range of community activities in Queensland and Western Australia over the past twenty years. Her current interest is in practice research and its role in contributing to frameworks and the identification of skills and competencies.

Carmel Laragy is a social work educator and consultant currently undertaking full-time doctoral studies at La Trobe University. She has worked within the public welfare system, and has taught direct social work practice in a number of universities. She conducts training programs for social workers and is currently evaluating a series of these. She has a particular interest in addressing the challenges raised by the need for social workers to work effectively within their employing organisational context.

Margaret Lynn has been a social welfare practitioner and educator for more than twenty years. She has worked in public welfare; child, adolescent and family services; and community development. She has chaired a regional consultative body and been involved in the establishment and community management of a number of community development organisations in the Gippsland region of Victoria since the early 1970s. She is currently senior lecturer and head of social welfare at the Gippsland campus of Monash University. Her research interests are in rural social work practice, and she is currently engaged in an action research project which explores diminishing networking across agencies.

Elizabeth Rabbitts is a social worker and author, and currently editor of *Australian Social Work*. In addition to her social work practice experience she spent several years as an adult educator with the New South Wales Department of Health. She completed a course for editors of small publications at the University of New England, Armidale, and has been conducting writing workshops around Australia since 1985. At these she encourages social workers to write about novel aspects of their practice and research and to explore the writing process in a relaxed atmosphere. She has a special interest in encouraging social workers to share their knowledge by seeking publication of their ideas in a variety of forums.

Martin Ryan is lecturer in social work at the University of Tasmania, Launceston, Australia. He has previously taught at Monash University and Victoria University of Technology. He has also worked as a financial counsellor and as a social worker in oncology and palliative care. His interest in practice research began with work on a Master's thesis on practice theory and occupational ideologies in financial counselling. He has also been involved in extensive studies of social work practice. His doctoral research was on consumer bankruptcy, and he has also researched palliative care social work and several areas in social work education.

Denise Sadique is a social worker with more than ten years experience in the field. She received her Bachelor of Social Work from the University of Melbourne, Australia, in 1983 and her Master of Social Work from La Trobe University, Melbourne, in 1995. She has worked in a variety of settings. Currently she works for the Commonwealth Rehabilitation Service in the state of Victoria. She has a keen interest in practice research, and believes it can enable social work best practice to be identified and articulated to the community.

Preface

Why a book about practice research, and why a reflective approach? Perhaps part of the answer lies in my experience. I have been a social worker for some years and am proud of it. It is an important part of my identity. I have also been a social work and welfare educator for most of those years and I am proud of that too. It is also an important part of my identity. The two identities are experienced together, and sit easily together for me. However, I have been struck by the continual tension between the worlds of 'the field' and 'academia', a tension which I experience continually in the attitudes of my colleagues, the policies and structures I encounter, and the related ideas which I internalise, often unthinkingly. This gap between my *personal experience* of my two identities as practitioner and academic, and the more *public expression* of the tension between the two worlds encapsulates for me one of the long-standing problems of social work.

How do we reconcile the gap between social work theorising and research, and the practice of social work as it is experienced by many? Although much of our social work rhetoric does pay lip service to the idea that practice and theory should be integrated, many social work curricula still persist in privileging theory over practice. Alternatively, social workers are exhorted to incorporate research into their practice, yet methods and approaches are advocated which bear little relevance to workplace demands. And why is it that social workers are castigated for not using research in their practice rather than researchers being castigated for their lack of attention to practice research? Indeed, why are not more social work academics engaged in researching social work practice? Might it be that the people whose discourse we accept in setting the terms of the debate are not those who experience the practice of social work? These are the sorts of questions that lie behind my decision to write a book that focuses on practice research—a book which showcases the experience of those actually undertaking the work.

I have taken what I have termed a 'reflective' approach, since I believe it is important to draw theories directly out of people's practice experience and that one way this can be done is through reflection on that experience. This is an alternative to the more traditional approach in which we have tended to assume that theory (or research findings) provides generalisations which then guide specific practices. In this latter view, the tendency has been to try to bring practice in line with the way social work is theorised, and to encourage social workers to use research in their practice (for example, Briar, 1990). The problem with this view is that it can focus attention on the deficits of the worker and her or his difficulties in integrating theory, practice and research.

A reflective approach takes a different stance. Instead of questioning the ways in which practitioners do or do not use theory/research, a reflective stance questions the ways in which theory, practice, research and the relationships between them have been formulated. This opens the way for alternative paradigms to develop which might be more congruent with the actual experiences of social workers. A small thread of writers has consistently argued that theory and research do not necessarily precede practice (Argyris & Schon, 1974; Schon, 1983; Polanyi, 1966; Kondrat, 1992; Peile, 1994; Scott, 1990) but that theory is often implicit in practice and is unavoidably integrated with it. As well, actual practice is often unpredictable and contradictory in a way that the conceptualisation of formal theory and research methodology tends to underplay. Any useful theory therefore needs to be modified by and responsive to the uncertainties of practice. Any approach to understanding social work should necessarily integrate theorising, researching and practising. A process of reflection on practice might thus involve the potential for theory development, research enquiry and practice improvement.

I am not arguing that social workers do not need to be taught about theory and research. However, my main point is that we also need to question how we learn to relate to, and use, different types of theories and research practices. It is this latter critical approach to which I am more clearly committed in this book. I believe it is more helpful to attempt to study the ways in which practice, theory and research are actually integrated in specific practice situations, than to concentrate our efforts on educating social workers to think and act in congruence with textbook theory and research. In this sense I am not addressing the issue of whether only particular types of research methodologies are compatible with social work, but am instead shifting the debate to questions of how we relate practice, theory and research. The view I take in this book is that practice research may be usefully undertaken using a range of research methodologies and techniques, and that no one exclusive approach is necessarily preferable to another.

I have chosen to focus on practice research (by this I mean research which is directly about practice, or which concentrates on applying the results of other research directly to practice) because I believe this is an area that needs more attention in social work. I have also chosen to use a *reflective* approach because I believe it can help the practitioner to uncover, articulate and develop the implicit assumptions that constitute one's practice wisdom. This book, then, is about theory, but not about the formalised sets of generalised rules from which we deduce specific actions. Rather, it is about the theory that we develop inductively from practice.

All the contributors are social workers who have recently under-taken, or are currently engaged in, practice research. Their contributions have been selected to illustrate a diversity of practice areas, research methods and designs. The chapters have been organised to highlight some of the key sites which pose questions for practice researchers—the politics of doing research with organisations, the process of choosing methodology and design, the difficulties of articulating actual social work practices, and processes of developing practice theory. The book begins in Chapter 1 with a description of the reflective approach and process, and ends by connecting the reflective experience with more formal theorising about reflective practices.

All the contributors have been asked to reflect upon their experiences of conducting their research in order to draw out the theory which has shaped their practice. Their accounts are therefore neither purely personal nor purely academic, theoretical or practical, but are instead an attempt to illustrate that the three worlds can be merged meaningfully to develop theory, practice and research that are relevant to the experience of social workers. The message of this book is simple: practice research is accessible, manageable and useful, and can be designed in a variety of ways to suit a multiplicity of social workers, situations, needs and aims.

PREFACE XV

REFERENCES

Argyris, C. & Schon, D. (1974) *Theory in Practice: Increasing Professional Effectiveness*, Jossey-Bass, San Francisco

Briar, S. (1990) 'Empiricism in clinical practice: Present and future', in Videka-Sherman, L. & Reid, W. (eds) *Advances in Clinical Social Work Research*, NASW Press, Silver Spring, pp.1–7

Kondrat, M. E. (1992) 'Reclaiming the practical: Formal and substantive rationality in social work practice', *Social Service Review*, June, pp.237–255

Peile, C. (1994) 'Theory, practice and research: Casual acquaintances or a seamless whole?', *Australian Social Work*, vol. 47 no. 2, pp.17–23

Polanyi, M. (1966) *The Tacit Dimension*, Doubleday, New York

Schon, D. (1983) *The Reflective Practitioner*, Basic Books, New York

Scott, D. (1990) 'Practice wisdom: The neglected source of practice research', *Social Work*, vol. 35 no. 6, pp.564–568

1 The reflective researcher: Developing a reflective approach to practice
Jan Fook

In writing this first chapter I faced a number of dilemmas as to how to construct it. I wanted to show that there are good theoretical justifications for taking a reflective approach, and I felt that unless I did so, the value of such an approach would be discounted. On the other hand, I did not want to do the very thing I am criticising in this book, to privilege formal theory over reflective experience. Upon reflection, I realised that the way I have arrived at my own personal reflective approach to my practice has in fact been through a series of seemingly unrelated encounters with particular ideas (those of Argyris and Schon (1974) and Dreyfus and Dreyfus (1986), and ideas about the problem of practice research); specific teaching and research practices (the use of the critical incident technique and narrative analysis); and the almost random connection of these with different sets of theories (adult education, feminism, post-structuralism). It has only been after about five years that I believe I have made meaningful connections between the characteristics of a reflective approach and aspects of other recognised theoretical frameworks. Therefore I have decided to describe the reflective approach along similar lines to the way it has developed in my own thinking and reflection.

PATHWAYS TO DISCOVERING A REFLECTIVE PERSPECTIVE

In the early 1980s I undertook some theoretical research into the possibilties of radical casework practice (see Chapter 11). I was

1

convinced that abstract theory could provide directions for practice, in the way I had so often assured my own students that it should. After all, I reasoned, if we do hold certain beliefs dear, then presumably (it follows logically) these beliefs will affect the way we act. So I unquestioningly adopted a deductive model, using the broad tenets of Marxist, socialist and feminist theories to develop specific strategies for casework practice. My mission was to demonstrate that it could be done—logically and rationally.

I had no reason to question this approach for some years. Students liked the model. They were ideologically relieved that their favourite theory could translate into practice. Here was a way in which students could be social workers and remain politically correct! Beginning students particularly seemed to like the certainty and clarity of it all.

In 1990 I became involved in some long-term research into social work knowledge and skill development through participants' accounts of their practice (see Chapters 9 and 10). Early interviews with both beginning students and experienced practitioners seemed to indicate that although many people said they believed in a particular theoretical approach, the ways in which they handled practice situations often implied very different assumptions. This was not so very surprising to me, because 'the gap between theory and practice' is a long-standing practice wisdom, and because a substantial body of research indicates that social workers tend not to use a great deal of formalised theory or research in their practice. While it was a little disturbing to find that our research yet again supported these findings, I still thought the solution was a simple matter of teaching social workers to better connect formal theory and specific practice.

However, one of the research tools that we used in our study was critical incident technique, in which we asked participants to describe an incident from their practice which they believed was significant to their development as social workers. In analysing accounts of these incidents, it occurred to me not only that we as researchers were gaining valuable information about what types of situations contribute to social worker learning, but that the process of reflecting on the incident itself was a learning experience for the worker. As well, it potentially unearthed all sorts of theoretical assumptions of which the worker was not always aware. Here was, I thought, a valuable tool for teaching the integration of theory and practice. At this time I also happened to gain a new position in which I was responsible for the coordination of field education. I introduced critical incident analysis to the formal requirements of field practicum reports (Fook *et al.* 1994). Later, when we were searching for an engaging way in which to educate advanced level field educators, my field education colleagues successfully incorporated critical incident analysis by using it as a basis for group discussion and reflection around student supervision.

At the same time that I was coordinating field education, I became involved in teaching one of the first Masters-level advanced practice courses in Australia, set up by my colleague Bill Healy. Bill had been interested in the work of Argyris and Schon for some time, and incorporated their approach into the basic approach of the course. This was my first exposure to an approach explicitly labelled 'reflective'. It was only when actually designing class exercises around the Argyris and Schon framework, wherein students discussed their practice and differences between conscious and implicit assumptions, that I realised that what we were doing was not so very different from the critical incident analysis I was using in field education.

My ongoing research into social work knowledge and skill development was also exposing me to further studies which seemed to suggest that professional practitioners, in fact experts, not only do *not* use formal theory but cannot even articulate why they act in certain ways. Some research seemed to indicate that the use of intuition is paramount in expert-level practice (Dreyfus & Dreyfus, 1986). This further confused me and led me to question the primacy of deductive theoretical thinking.

However, during all this time I still held my commitment to broadly 'radical' social work principles and tried to ensure that my teaching practice was congruent with the formal theory of liberatory 'Freirean' approaches and feminist perspectives. These theories formed the basis of my 'espoused theory' at this time, and to these approaches I added the principles of adult education, which were widely used by my field education colleagues at the time. I was aware that all these theoretical systems were vaguely congruent, but was puzzled that there seemed to be little literature that acknowledged more formal connections. It almost felt as if I were suspending my support of these theories while pursuing critical incident-based teaching and the Argyris and Schon material.

A colleague had suggested that we write a book about practice from the opposite angle to the deductive approach I had taken in my work on radical casework. The idea appealed to me very much, but in trying to develop a framework for the book, I was niggled by doubts about the theoretical substance of such work. The breakthrough came when I began to encounter the writings of feminist post-structural theorists. It seemed to me that there were parallels between the narrative, deconstructive and semiotic techniques favoured by post-structural researchers (Kellehear, 1993), critical incident techniques, and the reflective approach of Argyris and Schon. And post-structuralism, with the emphasis on the importance of subjective, interpretive and non-linear processes, somehow seemed to provide a theoretical connection which allowed me to take all these 'bits and pieces' and further develop them into a meaningful way of learning through experience.

So, thanks to a series of seemingly random connections, pressures of new job requirements, influences of like-minded colleagues, and discoveries from research, I can now present a version of a reflective approach developed from my experience.

WHAT IS A REFLECTIVE APPROACH?

In broad terms, a reflective approach acknowledges that, contrary to the idea that formal theorising precedes action in a linear (from cause to effect) and deductive relationship, theory is typically implicit in a person's actions and may or may not be congruent with the theoretical assumptions the person believes themself to be acting upon. In Argyris and Schon's terms (1974), there may be a difference between the theory implicit in action ('theory-in-use') and the theoretical assumptions a person might consciously articulate ('espoused theory'). Rather than using consciously espoused general theory in a *deductive* way to indicate actions in a specific situation, practitioners may in fact use, and benefit from using, a more *inductive* approach whereby a more general theory of how to act might be developed from a series of specific experiences (through a process of articulating the implicit theory).

In this sense, then, the use of *intuition* might be important in recognising significant factors in situations and making connections between seemingly logically unrelated experiences. This reaffirms the *artistry* of professional practice involved in the ability to make judgments to act in situations which are often unpredictable, complex, changing and uncontrollable. This recognition that situations can often not be controlled is related to an acknowledgment that no one universal or unified framework can be regarded as relevant for all situations, but that in any one situation, any number of perspectives might legitimately apply. It is important, then, to recognise that an understanding of any situation must be based on an appreciation of the *context*, and also of the different and possibly competing perspectives which might be involved in interpreting the situation. Any one interpretation of a situation, in this sense, is *only* one perspective on a situation and, as such, remains at the level of an interpretation of 'reality' rather than 'reality' itself. A reflective approach in this sense recognises that 'reality' merely consists of the extent and ways in which the different players share an understanding of the situation. It becomes important, then, as researchers and practitioners, to appreciate the situation in ways which are congruent with the perspectives of the players we believe are important, be they marginal or ostensibly dominant groups. This reaffirms the import-ance of a *holistic* perspective which takes account of the entire situation and context and the ways in which different perspectives relate.

A reflective approach thus rejects some of the basic tenets of 'scientific', 'positivist' and 'technical/rational' paradigms in their tendency to seek to understand and control situations by breaking them down into specialist and separate areas and trying to build knowledge only upon phenomena that can be empirically observed. Instead, a reflective approach affirms the importance of experiential and interconnected ways of knowing the world, and favours more emancipatory and participatory research practices. In this sense, a reflective approach blurs the traditional boundaries and separations between 'knowing and doing', 'values and facts', 'art and science', 'theory and practice', 'subjectivity and objectivity'. It recognises that in many instances these categories have been artificially constructed and often falsely opposed to one another, with one category being assigned more value than, or privileged over, the other. Instead, a more holistic and complex understanding (which might be a more congruent picture of the way some people experience their worlds) might be reached by blurring these distinctions and allowing for multiple categories.

WHAT CAN BE GAINED BY ENGAGING IN REFLECTION UPON PRACTICE?

Exposing practice to reflection allows for inquiry, criticism, change and accountability. Taking a reflective approach to practice means that the joint goals of practice, research and theory can be served in any one piece of activity. Let us take a piece of evaluative research as an example. There is potential, through reflecting on specific practices, to evaluate an action (a research goal) and from this evaluation to develop changed, or even new and improved, practices (a practice goal). In the process, a goal of accountability has also been satisfied. In the process of evaluation, presumably some criti-cism has been undertaken which might serve to refine or reaffirm some theoretical points.

Reflecting on actions, and the reasons, rationales and justifica-tions (a priori, ad hoc and post hoc) for them, may assist the practitioner not only to identify specific practices and theoretical assumptions implicit in her or his work, but also to articulate the basis for intuitive actions. From a research point of view, any contribution to the documentation and description of social work practice is invaluable. From a practice point of view, the development of practice theory, and the resulting opportunity to document, scrutinise, develop and teach the practice wisdom of experienced practitioners, is a boon to the profession.

The framework of Argyris and Schon (1974) illustrates the value of a reflective approach in improving practice by assisting professionals to align their practice with their desired theoretical framework. By pointing out that the theory embedded in practice ('theory-in-use') may quite often be different from, if not opposed to, the theory which is consciously articulated ('espoused theory'), Argyris and Schon have effectively constructed a framework by which practice can be analysed for contradictions between theory and practice. Professionals are thus able to pinpoint particular aspects of practice which may need to be modified in line with consciously chosen theory, or to identify and develop theoretical ideas in line with experience.

In some ways, a reflective approach offers in concrete practice what has been argued for in theory for some time—the actual integration of theory, practice and research. It serves to validate the experience of social work practitioners as a legitimate and important site for research, learning and theorising. There is potential for such an approach to be used for self-learning, supervision and peer supervision, classroom learning, research—in short, in any setting where social workers practise. It takes theory and research out of the purely academic domain and places them firmly back in the domain of all social workers.

THE REFLECTIVE PROCESS

I've developed a process for reflection on practice which I have found useful in teaching, research, and in my own practice. I have derived it directly and indirectly from an amalgam of ideas from Argyris and Schon (1974), critical incident analysis and technique (Benner, 1984; Fook et al. 1994; Cooper, 1994), thematic and semiotic analysis (Kellehear, 1993), and critical reflective techniques (Rossiter, 1994; Moffat, 1994).

1 Identify and describe the practice/experience and its context in terms as concrete and specific as possible. The practice you choose to describe might conceivably include any activity you perform or experience as a social worker: your handling of a particular interaction, your implementation of a program, a particular incident which occurred or one you observed. Your choice of

particular practice or experience may be guided by what you wish to learn from the situation. It might be a piece of practice or experience you wish to change, evaluate or simply understand better.

The *context* you describe should include details of any contextual issues you consider important, such as organisational, policy or community contexts, professional or personal issues, time of day or week, incidents that immediately preceded the one in question.

2 *Reflect* on your account. I have found the following questions useful in stimulating a critical analysis of my work. Some are more specific than others, and several overlap, but you might find that different ways of asking similar questions about your practice are helpful.

a What main themes and patterns emerge from my account?
b Try to differentiate thoughts, feelings, actions, intentions and interpretations. How are they connected?
c What interpretations or explanations did I make, and whose interpretations are they? How did my interpretations influence the situation? How did I personally influence the situation? How might the situation have been interpreted differently by someone else, or from a different perspective?
d What assumptions are implied in my account, and how relevant are they to the situation?
e What are the assumptions about? practice theory? human behaviour? value systems? political change? et cetera.
f Where do these assumptions come from? Whose assumptions are they, and who stands to gain from holding them? Are they mine and/or what roles/power positions was I assuming in making particular assumptions? Are they conflictual or contradictory?
g What are the gaps and biases implied in my account? What perspectives are repressed, distorted, or simply missing or de-emphasised?
h What actions or assumptions reinforce these gaps and biases?
i What type of *language* did I use? What are the *key and recurring terms*, and what do they imply? What *categories/classifications* are implied? Are they oppositional categories? Why did I choose to use these terms, and what others could have been used in their place? How concrete or abstract was my terminology, and what led me to frame my account in this way? What functions are performed by framing my practice in this way?
j What was expected and unexpected, and what contradictions are implied?

3   *Develop* practice and theory. The following questions may help:

   a   How does what happened compare with what I assumed I
       was doing or intended to do? Was the theory I thought I was
       acting upon different from what is implied in my actions?
   b   What is similar or different about this experience compared
       with other of my experiences?
   c   What further questions arise about my theory and practice
       as a result of this experience?
   d   How do my existing assumptions need to be modified, and
       what changed practices are implied by this?
   e   What alternative language or terminology (or categories
       thereof) can be developed to describe my experiences?

This type of reflective process can be used in a number of ways
and in different settings as a combined research and educative tool.
For example, formal class presentations can be organised around the
process and serve as a basis for group discussion and learning. It
can be used in supervision, either in group or one-to-one situations.
It can be used alone, as a self-reflective process. It can potentially
enrich professional practice experiences in ways that are limited only
by imagination.

REFERENCES

Argyris, C. & Schon, D. (1974) *Theory in Practice: Increasing Professional
    Effectiveness*, Jossey-Bass, San Francisco
Benner, P. (1984) *From Novice to Expert: Excellence and Power in Clinical
    Nursing*, Addison Wesley, Menlo Park, California
Carew, R. (1979) 'The place and use of knowledge in social work practice',
    Social Work, vol. 9 no. 3, pp. 349–364
Cooper, L. (1994) 'Critical story telling in social work education', *Australian
    Journal of Adult and Community Education*, vol. 34 no. 2, pp. 131–141
Dreyfus, H. & Dreyfus, S. (1986) *Mind Over Machine: The Power of Human
    Intuition and Expertise in the Era of the Computer*, Basil Blackwell, Oxford
Fook, J., Ryan, M. & Hawkins, L. (1994) 'Becoming a social worker:
    Educational implications from preliminary findings of a longitudinal
    study', *Social Work Education*, vol. 13 no. 2, pp. 5–26
Kellehear, A. (1993) *The Unobtrusive Researcher: A Guide to Methods*, Allen
    & Unwin, Sydney
Moffat, K. (1994) 'Teaching social work practice as a reflective process',
    Paper presented at the 27th Congress of the International Association
    of Schools of Social Work, Amsterdam, July
Rossiter, A. (1994) 'Teaching social work skills from a critical perspective'
    in Hesser, K.-E.H. (ed) *Social Work Education: State of the Art*, Official
    Congress Publication, 27th Congress of the International Association of
    Schools of Social Work, Amsterdam, July, pp. 91–96

Part I
Identifying social work practices

2 A first attempt at research: Surveying rural social work practice

Sue Gleed

The research project discussed in this chapter was the first formal research I undertook in my social work career. The chapter begins with a brief personal history, discusses the reasons I became involved in research and the assumptions I held, then continues with a review of the underlying theory used and the research process as I experienced it.

My research project examined differences between remote and urban social welfare work with the purpose of ascertaining whether those differences were of sufficient significance to warrant special attention in the education and training of social work students at Northern Territory University. Based in Darwin, in remote northern Australia, the university caters mainly for students from the Northern Territory but also from other parts of Australia. I assumed that the majority of students who were studying for the social work/welfare degree would be working in a remote area or servicing clients who lived in remote areas and was therefore interested in whether the course would meet their needs when they qualified as social welfare workers.

The Northern Territory has a population of approximately 140 000, about half of whom live in Darwin, the capital, while the rest are dispersed over an area of 1.35 million square kilometres. Darwin lies 4235 km north of the nearest major city, Adelaide.

PERSONAL HISTORY

I had worked as a social worker for approximately thirteen years before taking up my present position as lecturer at Northern Territory University four years ago. My social work experience has included working with unemployed young people, women and children in domestic violence situations, and adolescents in foster care; and work in large organisations such as the Department of Social Security, statutory child and family welfare organisations and hospitals. Although I have worked for large government organisations, the majority of my experience has been in the non-government sector, establishing, maintaining and developing services for small organisations.

Most of you who have worked in that sector are aware of the survival skills required to ensure that any program continues to function. Many programs have minimal funding and staffing, and finding the time and resources for research is not often high on the list of priorities. I had worked in such organisations but, although I had been involved in parts of other research projects—for example, I had collected and presented statistics to government departments and contributed material to government inquiries—I had never used that information in formal research of my own design.

In hindsight I realise now that much of the raw material for research was there: data collection was required by funding bodies to justify the agency's existence and ensure further funding. This material could have been used for structured research to improve client services, to assist other organisations in their practice or to demonstrate to funding providers the need for expanded services.

I had over the years toyed with the idea of further study but there always seemed to be something else to do, or else I was living in a place where there were no tertiary institutions. Much of my working life has been spent in areas such as north Queensland and the Northern Territory. Living in these parts does not preclude study but when the facilities are not available the incentive and cost of study can be an obstacle. Although there are now more possibilities for external study, the costs involved are still discouraging for many. The isolation of studying alone can also be a disincentive. Not having anyone close by to discuss ideas with means you have only yourself to rely on; motivation and confidence can decrease rapidly under these conditions.

My reasons for becoming involved in formal research, then, were purely pragmatic. When I started working in a tertiary institution I needed higher qualifications. You can argue about the merits of higher qualifications and whether these make you a better social worker or lecturer/teacher, but in reality if you want to be part of the game you have to play by the rules, and success in academia is heavily influenced by qualifications.

Undertaking a higher degree also seemed a course of action which would benefit me if I decided to work again as a practitioner. I thought the experience would broaden my skills base and ability to perform a variety of tasks in the workplace.

When I embarked on further study, which necessitated the use of research skills and knowledge, I was daunted by my lack of experience. Research always seemed to be something that other professionals and social workers in academia engaged in but not something that social workers in practice had much to do with. My recollections of research subjects taught at university were hazy but I had a vivid image of them as being difficult, foreign and removed from the realities of everyday practice. I know I'm not the only one who remembers it this way!

Another reason some women may be hesitant to involve themselves in research is, I think, that it places yet another expectation on top of other competing demands. By the time I decided I needed to gain higher qualifications I had a full-time job as lecturer and field education coordinator at Northern Territory University and a young family who also needed my time and attention. To think about research and the demands it would place on me was quite daunting. Would I be able to add another responsibility to my already full agenda? Where would I find the time to complete all the work necessarily involved in a research project? Were there other areas of activity I could 'cull' so that I could include research more comfortably?

I observed other female academics around me and noticed that they were either single, in a permanent relationship but without children, or older and with qualifications gained when their children were more independent. The issue of women, work and children is an ongoing one and I am mentioning it here as it was and is relevant to my ability and willingness to engage in the research process. At times I felt (and still do, as I am still working towards my higher degree) as if I were juggling too many commitments, so it was important to prioritise and try to adhere to the time and resources I had allocated to set tasks. In reality this was not always possible, as other unplanned interruptions frequently occurred and so I would have to reschedule or work at quieter, unplanned times.

It is relevant here to distinguish between formal and informal research. We all research in a casual way—observing what we do, its effects, and then modifying our behaviour or practice to take account of this. I had done plenty of this kind of reflective, informal study but had minimal experience with the structured methods of research.

So I felt I was beginning from scratch, although in hindsight this was not quite the case. When I began reading research texts again (there are now some excellent texts written specifically for social work and the social sciences), some of the concepts and terminology came back to me, some of it seemed like common sense and some of it still seemed incomprehensible.

UNDERLYING THEORY

'The purpose of all social work research study is to answer questions or solve problems; each research study is a problem-driven enterprise' (Grinnell, 1993, p.4). Grinnell sees research as a process which utilises the same problem-solving method as everyday social work practice. This method involves four phases:

1 Problem identification, definition, and specification.
2 Generation of alternatives and selection of strategies for problem solution.
3 Implementation.
4 Evaluation and dissemination of findings.

Grinnell continues by placing this method into a research context and divides the research process into six phases:

1 Selecting a problem area.
2 Formulating a research question and hypothesis.
3 Formulating a research design.
4 Collecting data.
5 Analysing data and testing hypothesis.
6 Writing and evaluating research reports. (Grinnell, 1993, p.xxii).

It was not until after the research project was completed that this edition of Grinnell's book was published. However, I referred to similar work (Dane, 1990; Monette, Sullivan and DeJong, 1990) and my own approach is generally a problem-solving one.

The problem-solving approach espouses that our everyday experiences are generally problem-solving processes. Each day we are confronted with problems we have to solve and this involves making decisions and plans and taking action. Solving some of these problems may be quite simple and not even involve a conscious thought process. Tackling others will require a thought process which necessitates clear, logical thinking and will include defining the problem, establishing goals, examining alternative ways of achieving these goals, setting and completing tasks and assessing whether the goals have been achieved.

Problem-solving as an approach gives the social worker and/or researcher a framework to stay focused and goal directed. What Grinnell does is to put that approach into a research framework, making the process logical, sequential and manageable.

Finding Grinnell's book after the fact reinforced my belief that we all operate from theoretical assumptions anyway, whether in our working environment or in private life. I carried out the research using similar ideas but not consciously doing so. From my discussions with social workers involved in fieldwork supervision of students this is often their experience also. Many times potential supervisors have said they could not supervise a social work student because they did not remember any theories—they just did their job. However, when we have discussed what they do in their work and how they do it, they often recall the underlying theories on which their practice is pinned.

What Grinnell's work did for me was to reinforce the theory and give me an opportunity to examine in hindsight where the theory required adapting or changing in practice.

PROCESS

Phase 1 'Selecting a problem area'

The topic I chose to research was the differences between remote-area and urban social work practice, and whether these differences were substantial enough to warrant extra or different course content in the social work degree being taught at Northern Territory University.

The decision to research the practice of social work in remote areas seemed a natural one, as I had lived in northern Australia for at least ten years and believed there to be some differences between remote/rural and urban practice. Being responsible at the Northern Territory University for the social work field education program had also exposed me to the difficulties social workers faced in these areas and the problems I experienced trying to access them for placements i.e. who would bear the cost of placing students in such remote areas.

The work of Martinez-Brawley (1985) and Cheers (1985), as well as personal contacts with researchers and service providers in remote areas, had also drawn my attention to the study of remote/rural social work.

My interest was in applied research—research that might prove to be of some use to myself and to social work generally in remote parts of Australia, particularly in the Northern Territory.

In doing subsequent research I have followed that same maxim of researching issues and ideas that are of interest to me and will be of value in my work or to others engaged in similar work. Given that some of the research process is arduous you may as well enjoy it as much as possible!

Phase 2 'Formulating a research question' and Phase 3 'Formulating a research design'

Finding a topic got me to first base, but where to from there? I read research books and social work research to understand the theory and process. It all appeared quite logical and sensible and not too difficult, just laborious.

However, that complacency soon evaporated when I actually began writing and tried to define the term 'remote'. I discovered there were numbers of definitions of the term and writers did not seem to agree. It was then that I realised this task of research was fraught with uncertainties and I needed to be clear about my purpose to overcome the multiplicity of problems that would be thrown my way.

Moving through the problem-solving process, I found that it wasn't always sequential and that I would be working in more than one phase at a time or returning to a phase I thought I had completed. The literature review provides a good example of this. During the entire research process new material is found which needs to be included, so I was constantly adding information to this section. Of course I had to make decisions as to how long the review was going to be and what information was relevant, and this provided the necessary boundaries.

Actually writing the literature review was another steep learning curve, and one which I have improved on since. Most practising social workers are accomplished writers in certain areas, e.g. report writing, case notes, minutes of meetings and submissions. However, literature reviews demand a certain style and presentation. I agree with Rabbitts and Fook (Chapter 14) that specifying the purpose and audience defines the style and presentation of any document.

Helpful hints on writing a literature review are available in a number of texts (Dane, 1990; Monettte, Sullivan and DeJong, 1990) but again, the skills of writing are gained over time and not easily described in a text. Combined with this, reading other writers' literature reviews is a useful way of getting a feel for the style of writing. What information to include and exclude and how to structure and present the information are all questions which must be answered by the researcher and not always easily. In other words the researcher is constantly faced with decisions which must be made along the way. The ability to make decisions and carry them through is an important aspect of research but one which is not always highlighted by teachers of research. This skill is necessary in most jobs and needs to be transferred from those situations into the research process through trial and error.

The next step involved developing a sampling plan and was quite

straightforward. Both social work students and social welfare practitioners were required as respondents in this research. Social work
students at Northern Territory University were sampled by using
systematic random sampling. Numbers of social welfare workers are
relatively small in the Northern Territory, enabling all those willing
to participate to do so. Because many social workers and welfare
workers operate under different job titles, skills of utilising networks
and resources were necessary to trace social welfare workers for
inclusion.

Phase 4 'Collecting data' and Phase 5 'Analysing data and testing hypothesis'

The method chosen for collecting data from participants was a mail
survey. The decision to use this method was made for a number of
reasons. First, questionnaires are economical in both time and cost,
which was an important factor as the research was unfunded. Second,
distances in the Northern Territory are great and respondents were
spread from Alice Springs (in the south) to Nhulunbuy (east of
Darwin), so it was not feasible in terms of time and cost to interview
respondents personally. Due to these factors, the only way of conducting this kind of research was by mail survey.

I was aware from my reading and experience that surveys do
have drawbacks as a method of data collection. There is a chance
that respondents will misunderstand or not complete all questions
and there is no opportunity to follow up with the respondent if there
are difficulties (Dane, 1990). However, because the sample size of
social welfare workers was relatively small (approximately 50), it
was thought that this could be overcome to some extent by the
respondents' phoning me or by my following up with a phone call
if surveys were not returned. A large number of participants were
known to me because of my position as field education coordinator.
I used Dane's 'checkpoints for preparing a survey instrument' (1990,
p.137) to reduce the problems involved with using surveys as an
instrument and included a covering letter explaining the purpose of
the questionnaire and inviting participants to contact me if necessary.

Although respondents in Darwin could have been interviewed
personally, this was not done as it would have biased the data. As
it is important to standardise the responses as much as possible,
surveys were sent to all participants by mail.

When it came to composing the questionnaire, I remember thinking that I should keep the number of questions to a minimum to
maximise the chance of participants responding. This was based on
an assumption that if the survey was too long respondents would
not have the time to complete it.

Having written the questionnaire with this assumption in mind, I presented it to a group of peers for suggestions and comments. Their feedback made me realise that in trying to keep the questions to a minimum I would not elicit the required information because the survey was too brief. After some reworking I produced a longer, more detailed survey that would give me the information needed to achieve the objectives of the project. I formulated questions by looking at the objectives of the research and wording questions around these. This was probably the most time-consuming and tedious part of the project but it was vital to get this part right otherwise the data collected would be of limited use.

You have probably answered a number of questionnaires over the years yourselves and this experience is useful when preparing your own. I needed to think about who the participants were, how much time they had, what I was trying to find out, and how to ask questions in a clear, concise manner. I also needed to 'sell' the idea to respondents, i.e. tell them what was in it for them. I think one of the mistakes researchers often make is to believe that everyone shares a common interest in our subject of research and will therefore be only too thrilled to answer our questions! This is not the case. I came across a questionnaire recently which was several pages long. I had every intention of completing it, as it was for a colleague, however when I read the questions I realised that it would take me at least an hour or two to finish and I had neither the interest nor the time to do it.

Collecting the data and analysing it were the next tasks, and they too proved thought provoking in practice. A response rate of 56 per cent was achieved for the surveys distributed to social welfare workers, which was pleasing. This was, I believe, because I knew many of the respondents and because many of them supported the degree at Northern Territory University and were conscious of the importance of producing social workers who could function effectively in remote areas. In other words, the survey had some relevance to them.

I had collected both qualitative and quantitative data because of a belief that research is not purely a scientific process and that human experience is not always reducible to measurable quantities. Our experience of the world is not simply objective and to collect information using only measurable data would deny this. Although the problem-solving method fits with the positivist approach, there is room for flexibility which allows for both quantitative as well as qualitative data to be collected and used. I don't wish to go into the positivist versus naturalistic philosophical debates here. Suffice to say that social work research until quite recently has followed a scientific method in the belief that this will give it credibility and a standing in the scientific community as a profession with 'real' knowledge.

This view is changing, and writers such as Grinnell are exponents of an alternative view: 'that social work research should follow no single approach but must be methodologically pluralistic if the research process is to have any valid role in the generation of knowledge' (Grinnell, 1993, p.38).

This view of social work research is similar to the eclectic view of social work practice based on the belief that it is legitimate to use different approaches in different situations. The key is to discern which theory, approach or method could be useful and how it may be used to best effect.

Analysing the data came next. This was a task entailing many decisions I had not anticipated. Because I had collected both qualitative and qualitative data I was faced with having to analyse it somehow, and as I did not have the use of a computer program I did it manually. This involved hours of sifting through the questionnaires and recording the answers to each question.

It was difficult deciding into which category I placed information. For example, when a number of respondents reply that they use counselling, interviewing and communication skills, are they the same or different? Or when they reply that workers in remote areas need to be flexible, independent, able to use iniative and be creative, is it correct to put these under the heading 'personal attributes required in a remote setting'?

Phase 6 'Writing the research report and evaluating research reports'

When the analysis was completed, significant results were observed, discussed and conclusions drawn. This part of the process was the most rewarding because it allowed for some degree of creativity and forward thinking. Of course, I needed to beware of drawing conclusions beyond the limitations of the data collected, to be clear about the difference between results and opinions, and to enunciate these distinctions clearly.

CONCLUSION

That first experience of research was for me an engaging one and has given me the interest and confidence to continue and develop in this area. It is an area of social work in which we can all be engaged either as academics or practitioners and it seems that, as social work has more and more to justify its methods and knowledge, it will become even more necessary for us to become familiar with the skills and knowledge involved in this process.

My research experience also confirmed my belief that research is about learning new skills, transferring current skills to a new situation and having the confidence to do this. I strongly believe that we are all capable of learning new skills and of expanding our repertoires. What often restrains us from doing so is lack of confidence or opportunity.

I am acutely aware that many of our current students have similar ideas about research to the ones I held as a student, and that such ideas can paralyse us into inactivity for years afterwards. As social workers we all require some knowledge about research because we will all either be engaged directly in the research process, be a part of a research process or be consumers of research.

REFERENCES

Cheers, B. (1985) 'Aspects of interaction in remote communities', *Australian Social Work* vol. 38, no. 3

Dane, F. (1990) *Research Methods,* Brooks/Cole, Monterey

Grinnell, R. (1993) *Social Work Research and Evaluation*, 4th edn, F. E. Peacock, Itasca

Martinez-Brawley, E. (1985) 'Rural social work as a contextual specialty: Undergraduate focus or graduate concentration?' *Journal of Social Work Education,* vol. 21, no. 3

——(1987) 'Social work and the rural crisis: Is education responding?' Paper presented at the Council of Social Work Education, Annual Program Meeting, St Louis

——(1990) *Perspectives on the Small Community,* NASW Press, Silver Spring

Monette, D., Sullivan, T. and DeJong, C. (1990) *Applied Social Research*, Harcourt Brace Jovanovich, New York

3 Undertaking the challenge: Using qualitative methods to identify social work competencies

Denise Sadique

Undertaking practice research was probably the most challenging aspect of my Masters degree. It provided me with the opportunity to further develop my understanding of the research process as a valuable learning experience and as an important tool that social workers need to be able to use in order to validate their practice skills to the community.

Before I had even decided on a research topic I identified a supervisor whose expertise I valued and whose approach to students I always found to be supportive. I believed that receiving support and constructive comments during the supervision process would be essential to my learning and ability to maintain my focus during the project. This was borne out in practice. Taylor says that it is important to select a supervisor that you like and respect so you can keep the communication channels open (1993, p.123).

DECIDING ON A TOPIC

My choice of topic came from my observations and experience as a rehabilitation practitioner. Two particular influences led to my choice:

1 *The humanistic approach* of social workers as compared to the more scientific focus of rehabilitation practice and culture and my belief in the value of the humanistic approach in achieving successful rehabilitation outcomes.

While working as a social worker in the rehabilitation field,

I observed the influence of the scientific measurement approach to practice, which can either encourage or shatter individuals' hopes and beliefs about their future. This approach often uses individuals' performance on clinical tests to determine their functional potential and their rehabilitation program (Sadique, 1994, pp.6–7). My concerns about this approach are described by the carer of a person with brain damage: 'Treatment offered is very "scientific" and inflexible. There is a lack of insight and awareness of the real human needs of the individual' (Health Department, Community Services Victoria and Transport Accident Commission, 1991, p.77). In contrast, social work values such as respect for the dignity of the individual and the principle of self-determination put into practice during a rehabilitation program can empower a disabled person to take charge of the process of learning about their future (Sadique, 1994, p.7).

2   *The need for social workers to identify, articulate and market* the competencies they contribute to the rehabilitation industry.

Epstein says that social work in rehabilitation must be able to respond to the market challenges of 'What is it that you offer and what is its value?' He also states that there is a particular urgency in this because of contemporary preferences for science and technology, which award social prestige and more material benefits to disciplines that model themselves after the culture of science (1990, pp.130–131).

I considered these issues to be challenging to the social work profession and important enough to maintain my motivation throughout the research process. However, while it can be exciting to undertake projects that you consider significant, it can also be anxiety provoking. Taylor recommends choosing a research area you like in order to be successful (1993, p.123).

My research questions came easily from my own practice experience as a senior professional. I did not consider what the impact might be on the social work profession if my findings did not support my contentions until I was almost at the end of the process. On reflection, I think this was probably a wise omission. I came to realise that the purpose of research is the exploration, the uncertainty about the results, and the grappling with the outcome to bring some new learning to light.

In the title I decided on for my research, I innocently included the word 'competencies', hoping that this would increase the applicability of my research in the current industrial climate. But this created all sorts of confusion in relation to the National Training Board's policies on competencies, to which I had not intended to refer. So beware, language can easily be misconstrued.

THE POLITICS OF CHOOSING A METHODOLOGY

I am now convinced that politics affects all decisions, as it definitely affected my choice of methodology. As a senior professional under-taking a comparison of rehabilitation practitioners, I felt a number of pressures in my decision making about a methodology. These were:

1 To choose a methodology that would be considered extremely thorough and beyond reproach in the organisation where I work.
2 To ensure that my approach would maintain my objectivity and not be considered subjective.
3 To maintain the credibility of the project.
4 To maintain my credibility in undertaking research in an organisa-tion where I am employed at a senior level.

I would describe these four goals as my 'espoused theory' at the beginning of my research. However, as in any learning experience my thinking changed as my understanding of the research process progressed.

While there are certain advantages to undertaking practice research in the organisation where you work, such as your under-standing of the culture and your ability to identify best practice, there are also questions to ask yourself. Some of these are:

1 How is your research related to your current position?
2 How will your research be viewed by your peers and your managers?
3 Is it supportive of the organisation's purpose or does it contradict it?

A major concern for me was that my research would be consid-ered subjective or biased given that I was a social worker. This view was also expressed by a social worker and one of the managers that I work with. My response to both of them was: Who else would be motivated to identify social work competencies? If practitioners research their own competencies, does it make their research invalid? Are practitioners not best able to identify their own competencies?

I have always questioned any researcher's claim to objectivity given that there is usually a subjective aspect to research questions and research methodology. During this project I became more com-fortable with the idea of subjectivity and less threatened by the scientific approach to research that focuses on the objective. This empirical approach suggests that the world 'out there' is a reality that can be visited and studied objectively. Social scientists are less concerned with the objective and more concerned about how people make and understand their world. Worlds are considered to be 'lived in' places which the researcher must try to enter. Hence the world is not described as objective but as subjective (Kellehear, 1993, pp.26–27).

One of the aspects of undertaking research in one's own organisation that I had not considered was the threatening implications of myself as a senior professional exploring participants' practice. This was highlighted to me by one of the social work participants who claimed that completing the research questionnaires 'felt like an exam'. I realised that the practice of health professionals was seldom actually compared. For the social workers, this was probably exacerbated by the fact that I was their senior professional and could examine their practice more closely. However, while it may have been more threatening for a senior professional to explore the practice of professional staff, it probably ensured that participants' responses were examples of their best practice. This augured well for the quality of the research data.

THE INFLUENCE OF THEORY

The research project also provided me with the opportunity to incorporate recent learning from my Masters degree course work into my research design. I was particularly fascinated with Argyris and Schon's view (1974, p.7) that when people are asked how they would behave in a certain circumstance, they often give their 'espoused theory' of action. Argyris and Schon suggest that the theory that actually governs a person's actions is their 'theory in use', which may or may not be compatible with their 'espoused theory'. I thought it would be interesting to explore this view and ascertain if there were any differences between what participants said they did in practice and what they said they would do when given practice examples to discuss.

While this certainly made for interesting data, in hindsight it overly complicated my research design. I did not realise how much extra work I had created for myself by expanding my research with this added dimension.

TO BE QUALITATIVE OR QUANTITATIVE?

I came to this project with a scientific quantitative approach from my psychology background, but while planning it I became exposed to the value of qualitative research. This was like awakening to a whole new world and new meanings that could be discovered through the research process.

I chose a qualitative methodology because it did not involve imposing a structured framework for validation but rather sought to generate observations from rehabilitation practice for further analysis. The data produced from this approach was rich in detail about practice (Grinnell, 1988, p.189).

AT LAST, THE METHODS

To incorporate all the demands I imposed on myself, I evolved a very complicated design for the project. Consequently, developing it took longer than I expected. The design included two parts and three data-collection instruments.

Part One investigated the 'theory in use' of participants. The data collection instruments included:

1 *Two vignettes of hypothetical cases.* These were presented to participants in written form. Participants were asked to answer in writing a set of questions related to each vignette. The vignettes were from the rehabilitation field and sought to highlight participants' case management practice and the attitudes and values participants brought to their practice. This instrument provided flexibility and an open-endedness suited to the exploratory nature of the study (Grinnell, 1981, p.302).

2 *A critical incident interview.* Participants were interviewed and asked to provide a description of two critical incidents from their practice and the competencies employed in each incident. One incident was to be from the participants' case-management practice and the other was to be from their discipline-based professional practice. The critical incident technique is described as going beyond descriptions of readily observable behaviour to gather data about distinguishing competencies which characterise outstanding professional performance (Gonczi *et al.*, 1990, p.47).

Part Two investigated the 'espoused theory' of participants. The data collection instrument was a written questionnaire which was sent to participants five days after the responses to Part One had been completed so as to reduce the immediate influence of responses from the first part of the study. The questionnaire asked participants to describe the competencies they contributed to rehabilitation practice. It gathered information and enabled differences between responses to be monitored (Grinnell, 1988, p.470).

I piloted all three instruments on a sample that was similar to the final sample of other professionals (that is, there were no social workers in the group that pre-tested the instruments). I found the input from the pre-testing helpful in gaining feedback about the clarity of the instruments and identifying any language or expression in the design of the questionnaire that could be considered to show a bias towards the social work profession.

During the actual research, participants appeared to find it difficult to answer any questions that asked them to differentiate between the knowledge, skills and assumptions they used in their rehabilitation practice. This was not foreshadowed by the sample of professionals during the pre-testing. It might have been useful to define these terms in writing in order to further clarify what was expected of participants. This difficulty was particularly obvious when participants were asked questions by the interviewer about their critical incidents in rehabilitation practice. Participants tended to generalise their answers across the three categories.

The critical incident interviews were all taped using a cassette recorder, with participants' permission. The purpose of using a cassette recorder was to record the interviews verbatim rather than transcribing them. This ensured that I could participate more easily in the interviews and that exact details could be referred to later.

Although using a cassette recorder was an excellent time-saving device, it presented other problems for me. I suspect these problems may be generalised to the use of any technical equipment for research purposes. It is important to be extremely familiar with the equipment you use and to double check tapes before use to ensure that recordings will be clear. Even when I thought I was familiar with the equipment and had checked the tapes before use, one of my recordings was very difficult to hear and another was so faint that it had to be re-recorded.

Taylor suggests that the chosen methodology for any research project needs to be tolerated for a protracted time (1993, p.123). I found the qualitative methodology that I chose, though complex, provided me with a great deal of interesting information for analysis.

In carrying out the methodology, I tried very hard to be as open as I could be. I did not want my own beliefs to affect the data I was receiving. However, when I presented the purpose of the research to participants, I felt more comfortable sharing my purpose with the social workers than with the other professionals. I did not want the other professionals to feel uncomfortable or negated by the process because I appreciated their contribution, which enabled a comparison of competencies to occur.

Stevens discusses the issue of over-involvement by the researcher with certain groups and possible over-representation of that perspective in the data (1993, p.163). I was very sensitive to this and I think it influenced my choice of data analysis techniques.

ANALYSING THE DATA

The world of qualitative methodology had provided rich, meaningful data for me to synthesise. The amount of data I had was overwhelming, as was the thought of analysing it. I was now very aware of the 'messier' nature of a qualitative approach compared with a quantitative one. I needed to find a method of analysis that would give some order to the information I had. I found trying to identify an appropriate method of analysing qualitative data the most frustrating part of the research process. I searched through the traditional social work texts looking for an approach to light my way, but they were disappointing and only increased my confusion. I needed an approach that was clear and relevant to data about practice and which would assist me to interpret qualitative data in relation to my original research questions. Unfortunately many of the texts on research appeared to be more relevant to a scientific, quantitative approach.

As a social work practitioner, I am mainly involved with analysing qualitative information presented by the consumers of our service. I expected that approaches to qualitative data analysis would be dominant in research texts. This was a false assumption. I imagine that this is partly why social work practitioners are seldom attracted to undertaking practice research.

As a practitioner, it seemed to me that much of what the social work profession has to offer the human services is qualitative, but I was concerned that without simple methods of data analysis these contributions might not be easily identified. I consulted my supervisor about this. She directed me to some social science research texts, particularly those looking at content analysis as a possible method of analysis. The text I found most valuable was a very readable book by Allan Kellehear (1993), *The Unobtrusive Researcher: A Guide to Methods*. Suddenly I had options to consider.

Kellehear describes content analysis as the act of developing categories before searching for them in the data. A category is then quantified by counting the number of times it appears. I felt more comfortable using this approach given its quantitative elements. Categorising the data enabled me to synthesise it in an orderly manner for discussion. Another attractive feature of this approach was that it was systematic, allowing for control of intuition and any tendency towards distraction and bias (Kellehear, 1993, pp.34–37). This deductive analysis enabled me to examine evidence of case management competencies and value competencies in participants' responses to each of the three instruments (Sadique, 1994, pp.45–46).

One of the criticisms of content analysis is that its emphasis on frequency suggests that each individual count is of equal value or importance. In order to give more qualitative balance to my data analysis, I also undertook a thematic analysis. Kellehear says a thematic analysis differs from a content analysis because it looks for ideas in the data being examined. It takes its categories from the data and is more subjective and interpretive, and thus overcomes the problem of viewing all items as having equal value. Using this inductive approach, I identified themes and patterns from all three data-gathering exercises as they emerged from the recordings. I did not use a hypothesis or theoretical framework as a reference.

It was undertaking the thematic data analysis that led me to lower the pedestal on which I had placed the concepts of reliability and validity. These concepts, according to Kellehear, do not address the nature of meaning, experience and power, concepts that I consider intrinsic to professional practice. As Kellehear points out, validity in science is subject to shifts in the culture of the science community and is therefore a changeable concept itself (1993, pp.37–42). The process of analysing the data helped me to review that part of my 'espoused theory' that valued the objective approach over the subjective. In my efforts to be objective and thorough, I appeared to have complicated my approach to the research process.

FINALLY, RESULTS AND DISCUSSION

I certainly achieved my goal of a thorough methodology. I produced three sets of data which confirmed my research questions. I was able to identify case management and value competencies in social work practice in the rehabilitation setting. I was also to identify case management and value competencies that were more characteristic of social work practice. I have shared most of my results with the social workers in my organisation, and with some outside it.

The credibilty of the project was never seriously questioned. My own credibility in the eyes of the social work staff has been enhanced. In my organisation, and with other professional staff, I am recognised as a person with research skills that can be and have been drawn upon. I have consolidated my research skills and feel comfortable undertaking research when needed. In these days of increased accountability and reduced funds for human services, research is a valuable tool for all professionals.

SUMMARY

When I began this research I had many reasons for holding an 'espoused theory' that suggested a thorough research design would ensure my results were beyond question in the organisational context where the research was undertaken. This was particularly important because I was undertaking practice research within the organisation in which I was also employed. However, research is a process of learning by doing, and I learnt during and at the completion of the project that perhaps I had overestimated my need to be so thorough.

The consequences of undertaking practice research within my employing organisation were not as I expected. I found it to be an empowering experience and I was given some recognition for the skills that I had used. I also believe that undertaking practice research enabled me to contribute to the further development of social work practice in the rehabilitation field, about which there is very little literature.

I believe the complexity of my project was also a result of wanting to ensure objectivity and reduce the subjectivity of my approach. I realise now that there is always subjectivity, especially in the qualitative nature of what we as social workers do.

By adopting a qualitative approach to the research project, I gained rich data even though it appeared messier to analyse. I discovered that there are some very interesting approaches to analysing qualitative data. These approaches can be clear and practical. They value the meaning of experiences rather than trying to quantify them.

In summary, at the completion of my research, I came to formulate a 'theory of action' in research that revolves around the idea of reducing complexity: 'Simple is better.'

REFERENCES

Argyris, C. & Schon, D. (1974) *Theory in Practice: Increasing Professional Effectiveness*, Jossey-Bass, San Francisco

Epstein, W. (1990) 'Rational claims to effectiveness in social work's critical literature', *Social Science Journal*, vol. 27, no. 2, pp. 129–145

Gonczi, A., Hager, P. & Oliver, L. (1990) *Establishing Competency-Based Standards in the Professions*, Australian Government Publishing Service, Canberra

Grinnell, R. (1981) *Social Work Research and Evaluation*, F.E. Peacock, Itasca

——(1988) *Social Work Research and Evaluation*, 3rd edn, F.E. Peacock, Itasca

Health Department Victoria, Community Services Victoria and Transport Accident Commission (1991) *Report of 'Head Injury Impact' Project Acquired Brain Damage Data Base Study*, vol. 2, Melbourne

Kellehear, A. (1993) *The Unobtrusive Researcher: A Guide to Methods*, Allen & Unwin, Sydney

Sadique, D. (1994) Social Work Competencies in Rehabilitation Practice, Master of Social Work thesis, La Trobe University, Melbourne

Stevens, L. (1993) 'Reflexivity: Recognising subjectivity in research', in Colquhoun, D. & Kellehear, A. (eds) *Health Research in Practice: Political, Ethical and Methodological Issues*, Chapman & Hall, London, pp. 152–170

Taylor, B. (1993) 'Phenomenological method in nursing: Theory vs reality', in Colquhoun, D. & Kellehear, A. (eds) *Health Research in Practice: Political, Ethical and Methodological Issues*, Chapman & Hall, London, pp. 112–125

4 Managing and measuring social work activity in a hospital setting: A quantitative study

Helen Cleak

The following is a description of a research journey that two colleagues and I made as a result of a decision to undertake a research project. It was originally seen as a management imperative as we grappled to maintain a quality social work service in a busy acute-care hospital in metropolitan Melbourne in the face of relentless cutbacks coupled with an increased demand for our workers' time. Now that the project is many years behind us, it seems useful to reflect critically on every stage in the research process in the hope that we, and hopefully the reader, will benefit by the practice wisdom gained from the experience. I will give you an 'unsanitised' insight into the struggles and decision-making processes as we travelled through them, in the hope that you will be encouraged and challenged to begin your own journey, knowing that perfection in research is aimed for but rarely achieved and that small steps along the way are valuable and make an important contribution to the knowledge base of the social work profession.

BACKGROUND

Box Hill Hospital is a 312-bed acute-care hospital in the eastern suburbs of Melbourne, a large metropolitan Australian city. Throughout the 1980s, the number and scope of social work services offered at Box Hill Hospital expanded but by 1990 it was evident that the social work department needed a better management system to handle increasing workloads and the diminishing prospects of getting additional staff. The imminent introduction of case payment into the funding formula for acute-care hospitals was a further impetus for us to seek better ways to describe and account for our social work service.

Substantial statistics were kept which recorded each worker's contacts with patients each month, but there was no way to determine any qualitative aspects of their intervention, including how much time was spent with different kinds of patient groups, what kinds of intervention were given, and so on. One of the problems of time management in a health-care setting is that social work services are often subject to outside forces (Sheridan, 1988). The flow of work is often unpredictable, with caseloads being subject to program and policy changes such as ward closures, admission practices and even the attitude of a referring doctor. The crisis nature of hospital social work does not allow workers to pace themselves comfortably. A sudden or traumatic death or the presence of an angry relative requires an immediate response.

Documentation of social work time is highly fragmented and difficult to count, which is a challenge for any management information system. Empirical findings show the remarkably short duration of communication events among social work services; in one study more than half of all clients had interactions with social workers lasting less than two minutes (Lohmann, 1983).

Despite the implementation of a series of programs such as a duty system and an allocation system, the staff continued to raise concerns about how they could continue to operate with increased workloads and no likelihood of additional resources.

In 1991, the management team of the social work department decided to embark on a research project which would link social work activity with the medical and social diagnoses presented. The generation of this data would assist the department to identify and then predict the number and type of interventions required for different patient populations. This would then provide the basis of a caseload management tool which would facilitate a more empirically based method of case allocation. Another possible outcome would be the development of social work 'benchmarks', or minimum, standardised interventions for different medical or social conditions. These would become the basis of improved clinical practice which could then be monitored through supervision and quality improvement programs.

Had all the optimal environmental conditions been available for such a research project, we might never have started. Undesirable features we faced included:

- Having to juggle the project within the regular and ongoing workloads that the research team members were carrying.
- Having no computerised management information system to assist in the collation and analysis of the data. In fact, there was no computer in the department and thus no computer expertise, as all our data collection and analysis had been done manually.
- Having no additional resources to support the research team or even the infrastructure requirements such as an administrative staff member who could input the data.
- Having no experience in applying for research grants and not even knowing where to look.
- And finally, having limited confidence in our own research skills. Although two of the management team had completed a Master of Social Work by coursework and minor thesis and the third member had started one, this research seemed 'different'. First, it was voluntary (we didn't have to do it!) and we certainly didn't have the security of guidance and professional input from an academic supervisor. Bev Taylor (1993) talks about recognising the difference between 'theories of ideal conditions and realities of transpiring circumstances' and I suppose we made a decision to embark on our research journey allowing for 'detours' from the theory of idealised intentions.

Message No. 1: Don't wait until you have the ideal research conditions or you will never do it.

PROCESSING

One of our important goals was to obtain agreement from the clinical staff to proceed with the project and then to obtain their ongoing commitment to the process. It was relatively easy to sell the idea because they could see that the reward for their efforts might be a case allocation system that was fairer and more equitable than the present system. The management team presented the proposal at a staff meeting and then used this forum to discuss and debate the details of the research design over a number of weeks. One major undertaking was the development of a list of the department's services or procedures and the definition of these outputs. It was important that this list clearly indicated what constituted a unit of service and contained precise definitions so there was no doubt about which service was being 'delivered' to a patient.

The second consideration in encouraging participation from the staff was that they be reassured about the potential benefits of the research, and not fear that the data could be used for accountability purposes. This sense of personal investment in the research became extremely helpful during the implementation phase when recording large amounts of data over three months became a real chore.

Message No. 2: Try to develop mutual goals on the part of the research team and the staff so that motivation and commitment are maintained.

As mentioned earlier, the department had been keeping monthly statistics for a number of years. We decided to design the research instrument around the existing data collection tool. We hoped this would encourage compliance by staff and reduce the time and stress of adapting to a completely new and unfamiliar methodology.

Message No. 3: Minimise the potential intrusiveness of the research by building on systems that are already in operation.

PLANNING

Planning the research from design through to implementation took about six months. As with all research projects, we started with an idea and then looked around to ascertain whether someone else had already had a similar idea and worked on a solution. Discussions with other hospital social work administrators suggested that they collected data to reflect the hours of service provided, frequency of patient contact and types of services provided, but time was not specifically linked to types of medical and/or social problems.

The literature search revealed a dearth of contemporary material but highlighted the numerous variables that needed to be included in any analysis of case complexity. Earlier attempts to develop workload formulae in Australia included the social worker's assessment of each case according to its level of complexity and perceived level of responsibility and stress (Prime, 1977; Truswell, 1984). The research team wanted to include this variable in the research instrument as it was an obvious factor to consider in any case allocation system. Other literature indicated a strong relationship between social workers' expenditure of time and patients' psychosocial acuity (Coulton, Keller and Boone, 1986; Hedblom, 1987). This included the patients' social problems as well as their emotional responses to their illness, together with their family and community support.

The outcome of our reading was the design of a research instrument that amassed an enormous amount of data, all of which was interesting but not necessary for our purpose. A computer is capable of collecting any number of variables but the data has to be entered and then analysed, which can confuse and frustrate your efforts to complete your project. Our desire to be rigorous in allowing for every possible variable that could influence time to be accounted for resulted in our almost 'drowning' in a sea of data (Levinson, 1983). For example, there were 52 problem types with a total of 93 subsets.

Message No. 4: Take the time for careful formulation of your outcome goals. You need to determine in advance exactly what kind and how much data you really need to achieve these goals and be realistic about what you can handle.

The concept of focus is a major consideration in a well-designed research project. Do not try to justify everything your department is doing. It is better to target an area in which social work offers a unique or valued contribution; otherwise target an area that is a high priority for your institution (Sharp, 1994). In our project, it would have been better to look at intensity of services within one or two diagnostic categories such as hip replacement or an oncology disorder which involved a large volume of patients and presented length-of-stay issues for the hospital.

Message No. 5: You don't need to and cannot possibly look at data from every angle possible, even with access to a computer. Select the findings that are likely to be clinically and administratively meaningful.

DESIGN

The design was a quantitative analysis of social workers' intervention with inpatients at Box Hill Hospital using a data-collection sheet which collected 25 different variables. The data was classified according to client demographic data with particular focus on the type and multiplicity of medical diagnoses and major psychosocial problems identified by the social worker. Data was also collected on referral source, worker time spent in case-related activities, services provided and some measure of case complexity using a case rating system adapted from Truswell (1984). Last came the identification of any specific complications compounding the intervention. Where data was missing, every effort was made to obtain details from the case notes.

Medical diagnosis was assigned according to workers' interpretations of the principal reason for the patient's admission as assessed from the medical record and referral information. Ideally the diagnosis-related grouping, or DRG, assigned to each case would have been a more useful description, but this was not readily available to workers because the department was not computerised or linked to the hospital's computer at that time.

IMPLEMENTATION

All workers (15) and students completed a data-collection form for every patient seen within a three-month period. This time frame was considered long enough to collect a representative sample while allowing sufficient time for staff to become proficient in the accurate recording of the data. Because the research team spent so much time devising an exhaustive list of possible variables, there was very little confusion or uncertainty among the staff as to how a particular patient characteristic was to be coded. Considerable time was spent compiling a comprehensive coding manual to accompany the data-collection sheet and many staff meetings were dedicated to training staff in its use. As mentioned, there was already a culture of keeping some statistics so staff saw the research as an extension of what they already did rather than as a completely new system.

The department borrowed a computer from a university to which we had some field education and collegial ties and used an SPSS PC software package to analyse the data. We also decided that the research team would enter the data into the computer program from their monthly recording sheets, which further reduced their need to put in extra time learning a new methodology. One member of staff who was interested in developing her computer skills offered to help enter the data into the computer. As there were 1478 cases and each case had 25 possible variables, this was quite a workload in itself and as we had no extra staffing resources, data entry took almost six months.

Message No. 6: Don't underestimate the time and effort it takes to move from project design to implementation and analysis.

ANALYSIS

As mentioned earlier, if the research team had been clearer about its goals and more focused in how it was going to use the data, the analysis would have been less arduous. Because of the lack of relief staff to assist with normal work responsibilities, the analysis and writing up of the results took an inordinate amount of time—over a year, in fact—and as a result, we lost a lot of the impetus and initial commitment to the project. One member of the team resigned and took up employment elsewhere and the department became preoccupied with other professional struggles as a result of hospital restructuring. The team continued to meet outside working hours but the timing was irregular and much momentum was lost, except for a flurry of activity when we decided to present our findings to a national conference.

Message No. 7: If at all possible, set aside or secure funds and personnel-release time to accomplish your research goals.

I was also a member of the academic staff at the university's school of social work, and this link proved valuable. As well as borrowing a computer from the university, we also 'borrowed' some technical assistance from the school of social work in the form of a social scientist who had considerable computer skills and was prepared to give the management team some help. Once all the data was entered into the SPSS program, he met with us to decide on what we wanted out of the system. Initially the program gave us results in the form of frequencies and cross-tabulations. From there, the team tried to analyse the results, looking for trends and indicators that were significant in accounting for social work time.

This arrangement worked very well, although it took time to familiarise an 'outside' person with the function of a hospital social work department and our own research objectives. Clear communication became critical during the analysis, as decision making for statistical expediency had to be made consistent with clinical meaningfulness. For example, a number of our categories, such as age, had to be collapsed for the bivariable analysis. The 'expert' originally devised four numerically equal groups but the research team argued that the groups needed to reflect clinical significance and purpose so that the group 0–16 years, for instance, could be used to evaluate services in the paediatric ward. In retrospect, it would have been expedient to involve our expert in the project earlier so he could have had input at the design stage.

Message No. 8: If using such a partnership, make sure that the technical 'specialist' is also familiar with social work practice.

FINDINGS

The dependent variable was time, which consisted of direct clinical time with the patient or family (V1), clinical support time (V2), and total or patient-attributable time (V3). In the study, time was categorised as being of high, medium and low intensity. The design of the data-collection sheet precluded our determining how much time was spent on which service, as linking a service to an intervention was deemed too difficult for workers to assess. The staff only recorded total time in the three areas outlined above and the reason for the service, classified according to the comprehensive list in the coding manual, for example psychosocial assessment, information giving, case consultation, practical assistance, referral.

The research showed that there were considerable differences in the time expended in casework, even between workers in the same team and working in the same medical area. The question was therefore raised as to whether discrepancies in time were due to the individual worker, the complexities of the case or other factors. Do workers modify their workloads according to their volume of work, their preferred mode of working or resources available?

It was hoped that the weighting scale would reflect number, problems and skills required. However, although definitions were provided for each category, the weighting of cases was designated subjectively by the worker and therefore open to interpretation. For example, the crisis team tended to describe their cases according to the crisis rating because their referrals came largely from the emergency department and intervention usually had to occur quickly. Thus the worker may have perceived his/her service to be of a crisis nature because of the pressure to develop a treatment plan even if the presenting problem was not necessarily acute.

The results supported the hypothesis that cases which were considered complex consumed more time, especially direct clinical time (V1) as compared with patient-attributable time (V3).

Although the data suggested that diagnosis was not a significant predictor of intensity of social work time, it became useful when linked with the types of problems associated with it which involved a high intensity of time, because certain psychosocial 'problems' tended to cluster around certain medical diagnoses. For example, stroke patients require a high intensity of time because they tend to have 'problems' adjusting to their disabilities.

REPORTING THE FINDINGS

Completing a research project, from formulation to writing up the findings, can take at least one year and more often two. During this time, many decisions are made by the team, particularly around design issues. When it comes to writing up your research for public scrutiny, you need to explain to your audience why you made the decisions you did and the underlying assumptions on which those decisions were based. We found that because of the lag in completing our project, we had forgotten certain pieces of the rationale on which we based parts of our design. For example, why did we collapse the four possible diagnosis categories into two? The answer was simply because the workers usually recorded only two major diagnostic groups so it was not realistic to complete cross-tabulations on more. In retrospect, it would have been advantageous to have kept a research journal or diary to record significant decisions as we progressed and remind us of the reasoning behind our decision-making processes.

Social work departments in hospitals need to communicate and share their findings in order to ensure the enhancement of their services to patients and their survival in the present climate.

Unfortunately, the research project acquired such proportions that when the analysis was finally completed, the significance of the outcomes was largely overtaken by other departmental priorities. So apart from one presentation at a national conference, the results and the implications of the research were not sufficiently discussed or debated or their outcomes translated into programmatic changes.

Message No. 9: Any research design must include careful consideration of how you will present your results, in what format and for what audience. The organisation of the data for presentation to administrators should be brief as they will not read something too long. As well, the focus should be on information that might lead to decisions based on the findings.

CONCLUSION

Of necessity, social workers should do research such as describing and measuring their service both for internal management and planning purposes and to facilitate the demonstration of accountability. Accomplishing these objectives is necessary to maintain the social work role in the competitive climate of increasing hospital efficiency. Although our research fell short of this goal, it generated interest among staff members who were provided with feedback in the form of empirical data describing what they were doing.

Throughout this research journey we were guided by our collective misconception that if our research were to have a public airing it should be academic and very original. We now know that a little step, any step, is an important move toward achieving these objectives. We also found out that research often raises more questions than it answers, but by staying focused and not getting caught up in collecting ever more data, the project can meet some of its goals.

A recent American article presents a rationale for reinventing the American university as, once again, a mission-oriented institution (Harkavy and Puckett, 1994) with particular attention to social work and the social sciences. It promotes a form of participatory-action research in which professional social researchers operate as full collaborators with members of organisations 'directed towards problems in the real world and . . . concerned with application'. It does not suggest that the community become a laboratory for experimentation but that a mutually beneficial, democratic relationship between academics and non-academics can contribute to the solution of significant community problems (*ibid*, p.313).

This research project demonstrated the important role that schools of social work may have in the development of practice research. Front-line agencies should seek to foster links with academic sites so that a clinical and technical partnership can be established.

REFERENCES

Coulton, C., Keller, S. and Boone, C. (1985) 'Predicting social workers' expenditure of time with hospital patients', *Health and Social Work*, vol. 10, no. 1, pp. 35–43

Harkavy, I. and Puckett, J. (1994) 'Lessons from Hull House for the contemporary urban university', *Social Service Review*, September, pp. 299–321

Lohmann, R. (1983) 'Information processing in social services: A review of project INISS', *Administration in Social Work*, vol. 7, no. 2, pp. 91–97

Nurius, P. and Cnaan, R. (1991) 'Classifying software to better support social work practice', *Social Work*, vol. 36, no. 6, pp. 536–541

Sharp, J. (1994) 'Demonstrating the cost-effectiveness of social work services', *Social Work Administration*, Winter, pp. 17–22

Sheridan, M. (1988) 'Time management in health care social work', *Social Work in Health Care*, vol. 13, no. 3, pp. 91–99

Part II

Research in and with organisations

5 Using ethnographic methods to research the work world of social workers in child protection

Gary Hough

This chapter will offer a brief account of some of the research practice wisdom which developed out of my attempt to understand and document the organisational world of a front-line child protection team. This research was formulated within a tradition which asserts that starting with the practice problems of practitioners may be the best way of not imposing theory on practice, and of doing research that is not simply about practitioners but for them.

However, at a time when social workers' practices are continually subject to rationalisation and managerial re-organisation (as if their practices were, in a sense, irrational or pre-rational before they came under the new managerial gaze), research which focuses on their practice perspectives may be becoming harder to do. Precisely because such research exalts reflective practice, it will be out of step with the contemporary organisational contexts of public welfare work, which are scarcely interested in the reflective practice of practitioners or the facilitation of reflective research.

APPROACHING THE RESEARCH PROBLEM

After a decade of working for a state public welfare department, I moved into teaching social work in the mid-1980s with an awareness of the growing gulf between the escalating managerial perspectives of head office and the community-based perspectives of the local offices. From outside the organisation I became increasingly concerned about the narrowing of department functions and the increasing dominance of managerial discourses and understandings about the nature of the work done by the department.

I came to share a belief that managerialism is not about doing the same things cheaper or better. On the contrary, it is concerned with doing fundamentally different things; it will transform and redirect services to make them fit within the understandings (and solutions) that the generalist managers plan to bring to them. But if this broad contention is correct, then it is also likely that the colonisation and attendant transformation of social service work will be resisted by front-line workers. Their grounded experience of the work will ensure profound dissonances and contradictions with the corporate managers' attempts to redefine the work as clear, certain, predictable and transparent. The workers will know what public welfare workers have always known: that the amount of indeterminacy and uncertainty confronting occupations which practice in the sphere of moral behaviour, social problems and human conduct will always be high, and that public welfare agencies provide a fertile breeding ground for organisational uncertainty.

In formulating the focus of my research, my key assumption was that the command model of organisations, with its notions of imperative control, had created significant new problems for front-line workers as well as exacerbating some old ones. (This is not to say that corporate managerialism has not also contributed some positive things; rather, that the negatives, about which the corporate managers are mute, far outweigh the positives.)

This view is consistent with recent research and analysis of state welfare work. Over the last decade, and particularly over the last five years, gate keeping and rationing have everywhere increased for social workers, and the emphasis on decision making rather than notions of partnership, on restrictiveness rather than on support, and on client control rather than sharing, has led to greater use of compulsory measures against clients, and to more social distance between workers and service users. In turn, the service users are increasingly likely to identify social workers with agencies which do not meet their needs.

I am not assuming that there has ever existed some sort of golden era in state welfare service delivery. To an extent, state public welfare provision has always been heavily bureaucratised and directed in ways that obstruct and compromise the service ideals that practitioners initially bring to the work. But in the current context, this trend has been substantially amplified as the discourses and technologies of managerialism have entered the field and tried to dominate not only the management or administrative domain but the policy and practice domains as well.

I chose to explore these themes in the field of child protection because this has become both an important area of employment for social workers and an area in which they have attracted widespread criticism. Furthermore, social workers' modes of operation have been under particular managerial scrutiny in this field of work, with calls from the managers for changed skills and for new and different training.

In summary, then, I imagined the public welfare workplace as a 'contested terrain' where struggles over the content and meaning of practice would be played out. Certainly I was expecting profound clashes between the view from head office and the view from the front line (or, to use a metaphor, the view from the palace and the reality of life in the countryside).

I stress that these views were not seen as being held in separate spheres. Rather, the central managers' attempts to increase the clarification, formalisation, centralisation, and proceduralisation of the work are likely to create profound dissonances for the workers whose practical experience of the work will lead them to actively resist its redefinition. This resistance should be evident in the collision of values and practice precepts in the workers' daily struggle to enact their practice.

RESEARCH DESIGN

My research was designed to develop an account of the organisational and practice world of a front-line protective service team, and particularly to address the key question—'How do the workers (practitioners) experience the organisational construction and definition of their work?'

I decided that a case study of one or more front-line teams would be the best way to explore these themes, and because of constraints (of time particularly) and the need to explore a site in sufficient depth, I further decided to study just one sub-office team and to spend as much time as I could with it. This turned out to be five months. The original case study design proposed: documentation of the formal organisational structure (policy and procedure manuals, practice manuals, workload allocation systems, supervision, recording systems, etc.); attendance at office meetings; examination of the office 'culture'; auditing supervision sessions (to hear context-bound, rationalised accounts of practice); semi-structured interviews with field workers and supervisors; and group interviews at which the team could affirm, reject, or correct the way in which I had portrayed its perceptions and understandings. My research design assumed that I needed to get a sufficient sense of context (by immersion in the site) before the semi-structured interviews could begin.

I have briefly canvassed some of my theoretical assumptions above; clearly, my research was heavily directed by theory. Stoecker (1991, p.101) notes that while research not guided by theory may be seen as merely a 'collection of anecdotes', we face problems in deciding the extent to which the concrete empirical processes specified by different theoretical perspectives are present in our case. Arranging facts and theorising about events require the researcher to build and rebuild theory through attention to process, using historical and critical judgment to assess which elements of the general reside in the particular and to what extent. In ethnographic research, data analysis happens coterminously with data collection, and, using the 'constant comparative method' (Glaser & Strauss, 1967), patterns and themes can be developed and tested both within and across cases.

WHY A CASE STUDY?

Organisations are bounded institutions to which one must seek, negotiate and gain access. My research approach required a long-term involvement with an organisation, an adaptive research design and a close working relationship with the organisation. Such 'fine-grained' research, which involves intensive study of the behaviour and ideations of small groups, has clear advantages over 'broad-brush' approaches which use methods such as questionnaires and the analysis of secondary data and which assume the study of organisations from a distance by researchers who may never experience them (Lawler, 1985).

Strategies of research involve choices between modes of engagement which entail different constitutive assumptions, epistemological stances, and favoured methodologies. If the aim is to concentrate on how the social world is constructed as a 'social reality', then there must be an attempt to get inside the process of social construction by building up descriptions of how human beings engage in meaningful action and create a shared world. Such an approach demands in-depth analysis of limited realms of experience through immersion in the contexts in which they occur.

This broad orientation is clear in different contemporary approaches to researching organisations. See, in particular, the approaches of Denzin (interpretive interactionism), Jones (life history), Smircich (culture), Bougnon (cognitive maps), Turner (text), Susman (action research) and Schon (organisational learning) in Morgan's (1983) volume on organisational research; in many of the approaches surveyed by Bryman (1988); and in studies of groups of social work practitioners (Satyamurti, 1981: Corby, 1987, Pithouse, 1987; McDermott, 1988; McMahon, 1993).

CASE STUDY RESEARCH

So my research design developed as a case study based on first-hand observation and inquiry directed by theory. To delineate the nature of the organisational structures in use I needed to make a detailed examination of the work *in context* (Crompton & Jones, 1988).

Case studies (whether of individuals, organisations, communities or societies), although they are as likely to use quantitive as qualitative research methods, cannot meet the criticisms of the extensiveness design advocates who point to endemic problems of objectivity and generalisability. In general the charge is that case studies suffer from a lack of rigour and an excess of bias, that there is no assurance of either reliability or internal validity, and that they are best used for exploratory purposes (Yin, 1984). Of course, these criticisms are founded within a particular set of paradigmatic assumptions and it is worth remembering that case study methods do not preclude the selection and analysis of empirical or empiricist data. The case study is a research method, not a method of data collection.

Accepting that all research involves a creative leap from data to explanation, Mitchell (1983) stresses the strengths of case studies in their promise to bring explanatory power through 'intensive' research. The ideal of objectivity and scientific distance has been successfully challenged by feminist researchers in particular (Keller 1983; Stanley & Wise, 1983; Oakley, 1981), who view the committed, self-conscious involvement of the researcher as a prerequisite for rigorous research. If participatory research is viewed as research 'praxis', then the researcher, in prescribing the events, arranging the facts, and analysing them, may turn to herself and her collaborators (subjects) to test for validity as the case study starts with a community problem and works collaboratively with the community on that problem (Stoecker, 1991).

Stoecker also suggests that case study methods are most appropriate for research projects which attempt to explain holistically the dynamics of a particular social unit during a certain historical period. They also may be the best way in which we can refine general theory and apply effective interventions in complex situations. And because of the richness and immediacy of case study material, case studies can help in the definition of abstract concepts and in the provision of their concrete illustration (Platt, 1988).

As foreshadowed above, though, I expected that the actual

contours of the project would become manifest and continually change as I encountered the possibilities and constraints of a particular site at a particular time. One of the strengths of case studies is their interventive potential, but it is also one of their drawbacks. Indeed, Walker (1986) suggests that case studies run the risk of becoming an unwarranted and unaccountable intrusion into the lives of others. If this is true about case studies generally, it could be a particular problem with the type of research I was proposing; the political sensitivity and volatility of my research focus were sure to make research of the type predicated difficult to accomplish.

ENCOUNTERING THE ORGANISATION

Writers and theorists of both organisational and case study research (Bryman, 1988; Walker, 1986; Stoecker, 1991; Van Maanen, 1988) all stress the practical, theoretical and political problems of access to organisations—the problems of getting in, getting out and getting back. The problems of access are well documented in the literature and have both practical and ethical implications.

Obviously organisational gate keepers are in a position to project imperatives and constraints onto the work and there are good reasons why we should expect them to do so. Crompton and Jones (1988) suggest that all of the time spent in the organisation and in gaining access to it should be considered as part of the research, and it is somewhat surprising that many studies of public welfare practice are mute about the process of gaining access to the research site (Corby, 1987; Pithouse, 1987). Indeed, many researchers seem to have regarded the problems of access as something to negotiate and get out of the way rather than as essential data which may foreshadow crucial research issues (Schwartzman, 1993).

As I recounted above, I had worked in the department in the past and was known by some within it as a critic of managerialism and an advocate of the importance of understanding the work from the experiences and perspectives of the front-line workers. I chose not to seek entry through a 'friendly' local-office staff member and to then seek permission upwards through the organisation. Both for ethical and practical reasons, it seemed wiser to be open about the aims of the research and to seek access formally through regional and head-office management. One of the consequences of this decision was that I did not get to choose the particular office in which the research was undertaken.

To the department's credit, it gave permission for research which it could expect to be threatening, and asked me to negotiate with the local office. From then it took a further two months of continuous negotiation to complete the process of entry.

The local management obviously (and understandably) found the research threatening and, while unable to say no, it passively resisted my entry. I was not able to meet with the senior team until three weeks after my initial call to the office. They could offer me only a ten-minute meeting, and it became clear that most of them had not seen the research proposal which I had forwarded weeks before. They were critical of the research and their responses ranged from unenthusiastic to antagonistic. Their feeling was that the field-work team (of fifteen) would not like the research. They said I would have to approach them at a general staff meeting, which would not be possible for another three weeks.

When I met with the field workers they were both positive and enthusiastic about the research. The seniors' attribution of resistance to the field workers carried over to other parts of the research, so that, for instance, the auditing of (even some) supervision sessions was vetoed because the field workers were said to be opposed to it. Again, they didn't seem to be when I spoke to them. The field workers and the seniors were obviously in conflict and my entry to the site, with the express aim of documenting and validating field workers' perspectives, reminded me of the interventive power of the case study, and the fact that the conduct of research is a social process which has to find space for itself in organisational contexts where information is viewed not as a source of understanding but as a currency of power (Walker, 1986).

Studies of groups deep inside organisations in complex organisational societies must *not* assume a rationalistic and cooperative paradigm of the social world; profound conflicts of interests, values, feelings and actions pervade social life and there is unlikely to be *an* organisational culture but rather several or many conflicting ones. It was not until I had been at the office for several months that several of the field workers confessed that they had been warned (at a staff meeting) to be careful about what they told me, and indeed several workers would only talk to me outside the office (where they could not be seen doing so).

Van Maanen (1988) has noted that ethnographic research can often seem like character-building confessional tales which rebound from an 'insider's passionate perspective' to an 'outsider's dispassionate one'. 'There is usually something of the "they made me do it" in the writing—limits being characterised as non-negotiable demands imposed on the ethnographer' (Stevens, 1993 p.53). The changes to the research design owe much to the contested and conflict-ridden nature of the site (which I expected, so I can hardly complain about its placing substantial constraints around the conduct of the research).

The other major determinant of what became possible was the office's involvement, a few weeks after the research began, in a military-style 'raid' on a fundamentalist religious sect, in which a large number of children became subject to protective applications. This affected the tone of the office (setting up a chasm between the 'raiders', who knew all the secret information, and the rest), it led to the cancellation of most meetings for a number of months, and it stretched resources so that I felt guilty about taking up any of the staff's time.

THE UNRAVELLING/UNFOLDING OF THE RESEARCH DESIGN

The amount of time I had allocated to the field work became increasingly important, not so much in facilitating my doing what I had initially planned, but in allowing me to become known at the site and opening up the deeper experience and knowledge that comes from a sustained period of engagement.

I came to experience the office as a demoralised, highly stressed, angry, frustrated, besieged (from inside and outside), scared, and suspicious workplace. The interview material yielded particularly rich data in which the language of the workers reflected actual work happening but in terms dominated by organisational imperatives and events rather than by professional or client-based needs. I had been looking for details about everyday work and practice theory. What I found was a version of that, but one refracted through—perhaps more accurately one constructed by—the organisational environment. My own experiences of this enormously powerful environment mirrored that of the workers—including feelings of powerlessness, self-doubt and self-blame.

The degree or extent of discord and stress made it clear, though, that I had blundered into an even more fraught situation than I had imagined. Because some people would have preferred that I were not there, and because of the consequent difficulty in 'participating', I was cast primarily in the role of 'observer' and was feeling a bit like a thief in their midst, trying to 'steal' whatever information I could. It was also palpably clear that I had underestimated the political volatility of the research I was proposing, and that my openness about the focus of the research meant that my presence was politically charged from the outset. I ought to have been more prepared for the collision between the democratic design of the research and the command model of organisation which pervaded the department.

The intersecting set of ethical, professional, political, technical, and emotional dimensions in the conduct of the research seemed overwhelming at times, and would have been if I had seen myself as a lone actor. Weekly meetings with my research supervisor had been built into my research plan and these became progressively more crucial in helping me think through dilemmas, and in affirming decisions to adapt the research design.

Some general assumptions emerged, and these crucially influenced decisions about how the research should proceed.

1 The office was clearly in crisis. There had been a high turnover of staff during the last year (indeed, seven staff members moved during the first two months of the research, although four of these departures involved secondments of various sorts). The raids on the religious group had a huge impact on this particular office with the OIC being hardly present during the four months of the research. Half a dozen other staff were also more involved in secret 'raid' activity than in their normal duties and most formal planning meetings were 'on hold'. There were also substantial divisions among the staff between those who were privy to secret information and those who were not. While the research design relied on going 'deep' into one site and seeking thick description there, the research clearly had to take account of the fact that it was conducted by *this* researcher, in *this* office, at *this* time, and this had a number of implications.

2 The raid imposed itself on the research and so had to become part of it.

3 The relationship between the seniors and the field workers emerged as very poor indeed. While I had been predicating clashes of values and modes of rationality between field workers and their managers, the immediate supervisors (both individually and collectively) might be seen as straddling, or falling on either side of, that divide. In my own earlier enactment of the role I had seen myself as characteristically siding with the workers and 'pushing up' rather than sending management imperatives down. It emerged that the supervisors' allegiances, at this site and time, were with the management side of the divide. By casting the research project as antagonistic to them (by warning the workers to be careful what they told me), management may have guaranteed that the workers (and one of the acting seniors) saw me as an ally, came slowly to trust me, and gave me some very potent responses in the interviews.

4 Because the nature of my participation was so circumscribed (compared with that originally planned) I did not have access to meetings or to worker supervision, and so had to rely to a greater

extent on the interview material (although this was partly balanced by the openness that the workers brought to the interviews).

5 The research process was also crucially affected and an open process of accountability to the group seemed not to be advisable or possible, because, while generally supportive of front-line perspectives, I did not wish to become a player in office politics. To meet with the workers as a group, without their supervisors, was inadvisable and almost certainly impossible. Apart from anything else it would have taken time, which no-one had. On the other hand, the workers would have felt unable to talk openly with the seniors there. Furthermore, the need to protect all of the individuals involved dictated another series of decisions.

6 Because of the volatile office climate, confidentiality assumed even greater importance, and I chose not to share the progressive research data with the staff as the research proceeded, or to report the findings back to the group for comment. For the same reason (the belief that people might be punished in some way if certain statements or actions were attributed to them) I did not publicly discuss the research at all until two years later, by which time nearly all of the staff members (including most of the seniors) had moved on.

7 I also decided not to tape record the interviews because the respondents might not feel safe to say certain sorts of things. I chose to take written notes as the interviews proceeded, and the interviewees accepted the reasons for this and seemed reassured by it. I also assured them that, in presenting the findings, I would disaggregate the interviews in such a way that no respondent could be linked to any particular response.

8 It became clear that contemporary child protection work is even more overwhelmingly demanding and problematical than I had expected. With the supervisors mindful of their enormously potent mandate (and injunction) to protect children, of the lack of resources, and of a wider organisational culture interested in results and hard-headed management, I came to view them as being as badly used by the organisation, as are the workers and the clients.

9 It also seems clear that the local management was using its power negatively, to obstruct the type of research proposed and the social relationships it implied.

10 While this office, at that time, may be idiosyncratic in all sorts of ways, and may certainly be seen as an extreme example of a dysfunctional organisation, I argue that this is principally a question of *degree*. I believe that the findings of my research, which I do not have the scope to discuss here, transcend my case example, and the particular case study certainly did allow useful theorising about the broader system.

CONCLUSION

The actual research methods I used show some very substantial departures from the proposed research design, particularly in relation to the research process and to the principles of participatory action research. In reply to this, I can instance Clegg's (1990) comment that organisational worlds will always be far more uncertain, ambivalent, contradictory and ambiguous than any natural scientist might expect to find in the laboratory.

Certain types of research are always going to be difficult and sometimes painful to attempt. I came away with an abiding feeling that I could (should) have done much better in carrying out this research. But perhaps that's always going to be the case.

In ambitious organisational research of the type described here, there is substantial potential for negative consequences for all of the actors involved, and I tried to keep this constantly in mind. In an organisation so saturated with managerialism, research that seeks to give space, and validation, to front-line workers' perspectives, experiences and problem formulations will be challenged and resisted, partly because of the social relationships and values it implies, and partly because such practices are becoming less familiar and so are simply not understood.

Organisational research of this type clearly involves an organisational practice; I was not coming from outside to research the organisation but was engaging in and with it, and organisational practice, no less than research practice, requires critical self-reflection. There are easier ways of approaching the development of knowledge about organisations, but we shouldn't retreat to non-contentious organisational research where problems are understood in primarily technical terms. In the statement below, Pieper is writing about research, although her warning might apply equally well to managing organisations. It most certainly applies to research in organisations:

> When reality is reduced to manageable units that are dealt with in unthinking ways to achieve the illusion of a control that can never be attained, the connections with real world problems are automatically severed. (Pieper, 1985, p.8)

REFERENCES

Bryman, A. (1988). *Doing Research in Organizations*, Routledge, London

Clegg, S. (1990) *Modern Organizations: Organization Studies in the Postmodern World*, Sage, London

Corby, B. (1987) *Working with Child Abuse*, Open University Press, Buckingham

Crompton, R. and Jones, G. (1988) 'Researching white-collar organisations: Why sociologists should not stop doing case studies' in A. Bryman (ed.) *Doing Research in Organisations*, Routledge, London, pp. 68–81

Glaser, B. and Strauss, A. (1967) *The Discovery of Grounded Theory: Strategies for Qualitative Research*, Aldine, New York

Keller, E. (1983) 'Gender and science', in S. Harding and B. Hintikka (eds.) *Discovering Reality: Feminist Perspectives on Epistemology, Metaphysics, Methodology, and Philosophy of Science*, Reidel, Dordrecht, Holland, pp. 187–205

Lawler, E., Mohrman, A., Mohrman, S., Ledford, G., Cummings, T. *et al.* (1985) *Doing Research That is Useful for Theory and Practice*, Jossey-Bass, San Francisco

McDermott, F. (1988) Managing welfare: An exploration of the conditions of action of middle-level managers in a welfare bureaucracy, PhD thesis, University of Melbourne

McMahon, T. (1993) It's no bed of roses: Working in child welfare, PhD thesis, University of Illinois, Urbana-Champaign

Mitchell, J. (1983) 'Case and situation analysis', *Sociological Review*, vol. 31, no. 2, pp.187–211

Morgan, G. (1983) 'Toward a more reflective social science', in G. Morgan (ed.) *Beyond Method: Strategies for Social Research*, Sage, London, pp. 368–376

Oakley, A. (1981) 'Interviewing women: A contradiction in terms', in H. Roberts (ed.) *Doing Feminist Research,* Routledge & Kegan Paul, Boston, pp. 30–61

Pieper, M. (1985) 'The future of social work research', *Social Work Research and Abstracts* no. 25 pp.3–11

Pithouse, A. (1987) *Social Work: The Social Organization of an Invisible Trade*, Avebury, Aldershot

Platt, J. (1988) 'What can case studies do?', *Studies in Qualitative Methodology*, vol. 1, no. 1, pp.1–23

Satyamurti, C. (1981) *Occupational Survival*, Basil Blackwell, Oxford

Schwartzman, H. (1993) *Ethnography in Organiations*, Sage, Newbury Park

Stanley, L. and Wise, S. (1983) *Breaking Out: Feminist Consciousness and Feminist Research*, Routledge & Kegan Paul, Boston

Stevens, L. (1993) 'Reflexivity: Recognizing subjectivity in research' in D. Colquhoun and A. Kellehear (eds) *Health Research in Practice*, Chapman and Hall, London

Stoecker, R. (1991) 'Evaluating and rethinking the case study', *The Sociological Review* vol. 39 no. 1, pp.88–112

Van Maanen, J. (1988) *Tales of the Field: On Writing Ethnography,* University of Chicago Press, Chicago

Walker, R. (1986) 'Three good reasons for not doing case studies in curriculum research', in R. House (ed.) *New Directions in Educational Evaluation* Falmer Press, London, pp. 103–116

Yin, R. (1984) *Case Study Research: Design and Methods*, Sage, Beverly Hills

6 Breaking the solitudes to improve services for ethnic groups: Action research strategies

Robert Doyle

This is a reflection on how community organisation principles and action research techniques were used to implement a community action program, through what was originally conceived as a major research project, to study access for cultural and racial minorities to generalist (or mainstream) agencies in the health and social services field in a major Canadian city. I conceived the project when I was senior program director of the Social Planning Council of metropolitan Toronto (SPC), together with three board members of the organisation. The SPC is a respected social research and policy advocacy organisation in Canada's largest city and largest area of immigrant settlement. The project may be seen as a case example of how research projects can be modified over time to become influential change agents in a community context; the outcome was to break down the situation of 'two solitudes' which characterises the relationship of mainstream and ethnospecific agencies. In this chapter, my reference to cultural and racial minorities includes persons from non-English-speaking backgrounds (NESB) and Aboriginal people, who are targeted in Australia by the Commonwealth government's Access and Equity Strategy.

ACCESS WITHIN THE HUMAN SERVICES SYSTEM

Human services agencies, whether under government or voluntary auspices, are the vehicles through which the community provides the programs and services to respond to human needs. Consumers need to have access to and be genuinely involved in these agencies and their services.

> consumers require services that are as accessible as possible on a geographic, psychological, or cultural basis and that afford them maximum choice. Their need is for accountability and effectiveness in meeting their problems. Consumers increasingly want to keep services and agencies responsive by having a strong voice in their planning and administration. (Perlman, 1975, p.101)

In advanced multicultural societies such as Australia and Canada, where the population has become multi-ethnic and multilingual, this means that consumers from diverse ethnic and racial backgrounds need to be involved in and served by generalist as well as specialist agencies (National Agenda, 1989). Unfortunately, there are few examples documented in either country where human service agencies have changed their policies and practices to adapt successfully to the multicultural reality of their communities. For example, a recent evaluation of the Australian government's Access and Equity Strategy (Jupp, 1992; Doyle, 1993) does not give an enthusiastic endorsement that government agencies have made widespread changes to promote access and equity for NESB and Aboriginal populations.

The action research project I will discuss was initiated out of a concern that people from cultural and racial minority groups were being 'ghettoised' and excluded from mainstream agencies set up to serve everyone, and that mainstream agencies were failing to adapt their structures and services to provide genuine access and equity. As initiators of the project, we saw the staff of mainstream agencies refusing to deal with clients from ethnic communities but eager and willing to refer them to ethnospecific agencies because 'they can understand ethnics there' and 'they can speak their language'. The development of ethnic ghettos was not tolerable in a community such as Toronto, which saw itself as a model for the multicultural society. The initial aim of the research (Doyle & Visano, 1987a, 1987b) was to analyse the problems of access for members of cultural and racial groups to mainstream health and social services in metropolitan Toronto, and make recommendations for change. In the study, 'mainstream' refers to agencies that offer services to everyone in the community who meets general eligibility criteria, regardless of membership in a particular cultural or racial group. In contrast, 'ethnic' or 'ethnospecific' refers to agencies which provide services to people on the basis of general criteria that emphasise membership in a particular cultural or racial group. While some people have difficulty accepting terminology which separates mainstream from ethnospecific agencies, it was felt that this represents the reality of the present service systems. Mainstream agencies are agencies which are designed to serve everyone (within the boundaries of their eligibility criteria) while ethnospecific agencies are designed to serve specific cultural and/or language groups.

GRAPPLING WITH THE CONCEPT OF ACCESS

Our first challenge as a group of researchers was to develop a clear definition of what we were studying. The concept of access defies simplistic definitions. At the outset of our research we saw that access incorporates both direct client services and organisational participation (i.e. access and participation). We defined 'client access' as the extent to which consumers are able to secure needed services, while 'organisational access' refers to the level of representation and/or participation in the planning, development, delivery and administration of those services (including employment as staff, representation on boards or committees of management, or participation as volunteers). The organisational component of access particularly relates to the purposes and effectiveness of service agencies which claim to reflect the diversity of communities they serve and to be culturally sensitive to consumers who seek their help.

Access and equity within the health and social services, particularly for minority populations, has been a largely neglected area, even though many studies have noted that people who need and are entitled to human services generally do not receive them in an equitable manner. Kahn (1973, p.31) states, for example, that lack of access may be due to factors such as the complexity and bureaucratic nature of the service system; discrimination; variations among citizens in knowledge and understanding of rights or in appreciation of the values of certain resources, benefits and entitlements; and the geographical distance between people and services.

When members of racial and cultural groups seek help from health and social services agencies they often have access problems which are common to other consumers but are more intense or more acute for them. They face, for example:

- limited knowledge of their rights and entitlements;
- personal and systemic discrimination;
- limited language ability, which makes it more difficult for them to secure services;
- cultural differences which can result in misconceptions and negative judgments from within agencies.

Members of minority groups face additional barriers because of language and culture. They are often bewildered by the vast and changing array of agency programs and services, and few are aware of their entitlements to services and the ways they can access those services. As I noted above, only a small number of service organisations in countries such as Australia and Canada have sufficiently changed their structures and operations to facilitate access to their structures, programs and services. Most human services agencies in developed countries with multicultural policies have not moved beyond 'monocultural' or 'ethnic-targeted' approaches (Liffman,1981; Tator, 1990) to dealing with the new multicultural reality in their communities. For example, such a situation obtains in agencies serving the elderly in Australia (Foster & Kendig, 1987) and in Canada (Ethnicity and Aging, 1988). Generalist or mainstream agencies which are required to provide universal access to their services must, for a variety of social justice and self-serving reasons, begin to undergo organisational change to equitably serve diverse multicultural populations.

THE ORIGINAL RESEARCH APPROACH

Our original research design was a fairly conventional one and grew out of a community-wide consultation process which provided support and encouragement for the SPC to carry out the project; funding was secured from the federal government. The primary research method was to be surveys of key personnel from mainstream agencies. Our debate at the outset was whether to survey agencies or consumers of services. We concluded that it was more appropriate and strategic to survey agencies. First, we felt that we needed to document the perceptions of agencies themselves as a first step to change rather than subject them to a consumer evaluation; second, we wanted agencies to be collaborators in the process and not 'get them offside' in the change process. After considerable debate in the council, we decided to maintain the survey focus on mainstream agencies but to also introduce a more balanced focus with some interviews with consumers as well as key informants from ethnic agencies and advocacy groups.

Interviews were held with respondents in 135 mainstream organisations, using two survey instruments. A 'face-to-face' questionnaire obtained perceptions on five types of barriers to access (information and awareness, physical and geographical, cultural, administrative, and cost); specific measures or strategies that organisations had taken to improve access; and ones which respondents felt should be taken in the overall system of services. A 'self-administered' questionnaire was left with respondents to collect data on their organisations regarding the existence of 'multicultural' policies and measures, composition of the staff and board, language and other information. Forty interviews were held with key informants involved with ethnospecific organisations; in addition, 160 interviews were held in six languages with consumers of services.

LEARNING AS YOU GO

Taking a community development approach

Coming from a community organisation background, my interest in incorporating action research principles into the design was shared by several colleagues. We felt that although the SPC was known for its research and advocacy work, these functions were not interrelated in its project work. Research was seen to be a more or less 'objective' and 'rational or analytic' process which should be persuasive to decision makers because of its quality; however, the divorce from 'community action' laid the research open to being ignored after the initial media flurry of reporting. To remedy this, we began to build the project on a community development model, emphasising the broadest possible participation of all interests or constituencies in the access issue. This meant that providers representing both ethnic (ethnospecific) and mainstream agencies, representatives from ethnocultural communities, consumers and funders needed to be involved as stakeholders in all aspects of the project.

Setting up advisory and consultative structures

To begin to involve some of these key interests in the process, we decided to set up a couple of structures to guide the implementation of the project. Representatives from 25 key agencies, mainly ethnospecific, who had been consulted during the design phase were invited to sit as a community advisory group (CAG). The CAG was to be our main point of reference throughout the conduct of the project. We then began to consider how we should relate to all those government agencies whose policies and funding make such a difference to how services agencies operate and systems are maintained.

We recollected that governments incessantly consult community representatives about all kinds of issues, although there is flimsy evidence that they take heed of this community advice in their decisions. We decided to 'turn the tables' and consult government agencies. We would seek their advice on our own terms, and be free to accept, reject or ignore it. We therefore established a government consultation group (GCG) of representatives from twelve government agencies at three levels (federal, provincial/state and municipal), all of whom were involved in funding services to ethnic consumers. Discussions with the GCG led to a decision to conduct a review of government funding policies and programs as a context for the anticipated findings from the interviews.

Using action research techniques

As we proceeded, we began to more fully appreciate the techniques of action research. While community work principles oriented us to involve all stakeholders, action research design helped us to get more specific about how to do this within our research. We noted that participatory research views all stakeholders as a 'participatory research collective' which makes up the research sample (Alary, p.245). As a result, we decided to engage some of the agencies in the sample and help them document some best-practice examples through case studies. These agencies were doing innovative work in providing access to cultural and racial minorities, ranging from innovative staff training programs to consulting with ethnic communities in the design of programs and services. In addition, we successfully negotiated with members of the GCG for the opportunity to jointly review the multicultural policies of their departments. Both the case studies and policy reviews would be part of the database for a full review of the state of access within the services system.

STUDY FINDINGS AND CONCLUSIONS

At this point, it might be helpful to report on the findings of the surveys. It was found that few mainstream organisations devoted much energy to making changes beyond the identification of barriers. While service providers expressed a sensitive appreciation of the problems for minorities involved in securing access, the results were disturbing in terms of the actual accomplishment or adoption of specific measures to reduce barriers.

Serious gaps were revealed in the information base of agencies regarding the cultural and racial characteristics of their clientele and workforce, including board and volunteer representation. Many agencies just did not know or care who they were serving—or, in this case, who they were not serving. Indeed, there seemed to be a poverty of ideas regarding what to do to confront barriers and obstacles to serving the needs of consumers. General conclusions drawn from the findings included:

- agencies recognise that barriers to access exist, and can list them;
- agencies experience difficulties in responding to barriers, and are unable to devise strategies and programs to effectively address these barriers;
- cost is a factor that has to be considered in order to improve

access, but it must be acknowledged that some changes to improve access may not entail any additional costs for agencies;
- change efforts within individual agencies are necessary but not sufficient to ensure the necessary system improvements;
- collective responses on the part of service agencies, rather than isolated solutions, are required to achieve more equitable access for minority groups.

Key informants felt that mainstream agencies do not effectively respond to the new multicultural reality, while the burden for ensuring access falls on smaller, more poorly funded and understaffed ethnospecific agencies. The surveys found that mainstream and ethnospecific organisations seem to operate in separate systems and compete for scarce resources.

Interviews confirmed that a majority of consumers from ethnocultural minorities experienced difficulties in securing access. However, they tended to attribute obstacles to factors such as lack of information, styles and techniques of interaction, and lack of knowledge and understanding of cultural and linguistic factors, which complicate delivery patterns. Consumers expressed feelings of uncertainty, powerlessness and distance from agencies set up to serve them. It was found that cultural factors either keep consumers from approaching agencies or effectively limit the value of assistance offered to them which doesn't recognise the particular values of consumers. Although consumers gave good assessments to agencies, they were critical of the staff and the services obtained. The most frequent criticism directed at staff concerns sensitivity—their failure to appreciate the predicament experienced by newcomers from different cultures.

Additions to the design

We noted that agencies, even if they wanted to take some action to increase access for minorities, seemed to have a poverty of ideas; they just did not seem to know specifically what to do about breaking the barriers that they had already identified. We had already included documenting case examples as kinds of best practice which might provide experience for agencies wanting guidelines for action on access issues.

Before publication of the research, we also decided to use the initial findings as a method for discussion and collaborative planning. Therefore, in cooperation with the CAG, we convened focus groups to review initial findings in the six municipalities of metropolitan Toronto. These focus groups provided opportunities to prepare some outlines of what the system of services should look like if equitable access for cultural and racial minorities was achieved.

A community program of action

The project found little evidence of overt discrimination based on race or culture, but access to services and institutional structures was seriously lacking. And while individual agencies or respondents were unable to provide substantive ideas for action, the case studies and focus groups contributed to what we began to see as a comprehensive program to improve access for cultural and racial minorities.

The earlier observation that mainstream and ethnospecific agencies operate as separate systems led me to consider the systems as 'two solitudes', a term used decades before to characterise the relationship between the English and French as the two founding nations of Canada (leaving aside the disengagement of the indigenous people, the First Nations). I wrote:

> As we proceeded in the study, it became apparent that the health and social services 'system', at least for members of diverse cultural and racial groups, could be characterised as a situation of 'two solitudes'. Rather than one system, there appear to be two systems (one might call them sub-systems), mainstream and ethnospecific, that exist side by side, live somewhat separate existences, hardly take account of one another in their efforts to plan and deliver services, and do not account to one another for their plans or activities.
>
> The analogy may be simplistically made to a married couple whose marriage has broken down, who share the same space and continue to have similar interests, but who no longer communicate with one another. The similarity ends there, however, as such a married couple once saw themselves as equal partners in a common cause, contracting with one another through their marriage vows to accomplish their common objectives.
>
> The prevailing nature, however, of the two solitudes is one where a partnership has never been formed. It is one where the mainstream system has never recognised the legitimacy of the ethnospecific system, seeing its value as being mainly to provide interpreter service or a referral source for a clientele the mainstream organisation cannot understand; and where the ethnospecific system, feeling besieged with a clientele who they believe should be served by mainstream organisations, ignores these organisations for the most part, preferring to interact with government agencies who in their view at least accept some limited responsibility for serving members of diverse cultural and racial groups.
>
> It is this condition of 'two solitudes' which must be addressed if members of minority groups are to have equitable access to the health and social services provided by mainstream and ethnospecific organisations for citizens in the metropolitan area.

To remedy this condition, we developed a program for change at four levels: at the individual agency or intra-organisational level (organisational changes within individual agencies); at the inter-organisational level (relationships between/among agencies); at the systemic level; and at the overall societal level.

The recommendations for change at the organisational level were considered to be particularly important as they seek to introduce fundamental changes in the way existing agencies and organisations deal with cultural and racial minorities. It is necessary to have examples of community agencies which are in the vanguard of multicultural change, as we need to learn from one another, and should not have to re-invent the wheel.

Action to increase access to services for members of cultural and racial groups requires that both ethnospecific and mainstream organisations are mobilised and work collaboratively. In effect, mainstream organisations need to see ethnospecific organisations as service partners and not simply as resources for translation and interpretation. And any effective program for action, i.e. a sense of interrelated and directed activities, requires a collaborative relationship between organisations in the two systems.

The program for action made recommendations for change in a variety of areas, such as community outreach, recruitment, personnel administration, communications, training and education, policies, programs and services; it gave attention to such matters as board and staff recruitment, translation and interpretation, outreach to minority communities, bilingual and multilingual staffing, case management, and others. It was emphasised that there is no panacea that will ensure access and equity—no one measure, such as training, that is sufficient for the extent of change required to make a difference for disadvantaged consumers. Rather, many initiatives are required to variously address changes in individual organisations such as information, recruitment and representation, services and programs; in the linkages between organisations; in funding policy and programs; in educational institutions and curricula; and in public education.

UTILITY OF THE APPROACH

The community development approach turned out to be the key ingredient in the project and made the research spring to life for both the participants and the community as a whole.

Government consultation group

For the government participants, their involvement in the GCG was productive. They were consulted on four occasions during the project, had an opportunity to be involved in the design, and reviewed the report's findings and recommendations before its public release. As a result, they developed their own strategies to build support in their respective departments and ministries. They set up internal government meetings to educate other staff, mobilised responses to the recommendations from within their departments and were the key internal actors who influenced government action on access issues. As such, they may be correctly seen as guerrillas in the bureaucracy.

One of the main outcomes of the project was to convince three large funders to take funding initiatives to promote access for cultural and racial minorities. The major provincial government agency took up the challenge of the project to establish a joint initiatives project, which funds joint proposals from mainstream and ethnospecific agency partners. The municipality of metropolitan Toronto (covering the six municipalities) set up an access fund to assist agencies to make efforts in access, while the United Way of Greater Toronto (the main non-government funder) organised a multicultural access project which supported a small number of agencies in undertaking multicultural change and then assisting other agencies to take similar steps.

Community advisory group

As the report was to be released, the members of the CAG decided to change from an advisory status to one with more direct responsibility for active follow-up on access issues and recommendations of the report. They co-sponsored (with the SPC) a community forum to publicly release the report, to do leadership work on its dissemination and to use it for public discussion and social action. One of the important recognitions was that the SPC report, although carried out by one voluntary or non-government organisation, was in the public realm and, in a real sense, belonged to the community.

The CAG developed into the Access Action Council (AAC), an autonomous organisation dedicated to pursuing equitable access to human services for members of cultural and racial minorities. The AAC's membership included representatives of both mainstream and ethnospecific agencies; in this way it could begin to build bridges between agencies in both sub-systems and be an important forum for community-wide debate and action on access issues. The AAC has now been in operation for almost seven years and has been in the forefront of community monitoring of government initiatives as well as in community education and advocacy on access issues. Its efforts have ranged from holding major conferences (for example, involving the ethnic elderly), to working on issues of police–minority relations, access to trades and professions, joint projects with two universities to undertake outreach to ethnic communities, and efforts to maintain innovation in access provision within mainstream agencies.

ELEMENTS OF A STRATEGY

Having explained how we undertook our research and re-formed our project, I will now identify some elements of the strategy which seemed to assure more equitable access within the human services for members of cultural and racial minorities.

Involving stakeholders in the process

The community development approach, involving participants in a variety of ways throughout the research process, was the most important ingredient for the project's success. Participants were involved in diagnosing problems, collecting information to make the necessary changes and evaluating the effectiveness of changes recommended, and they became advocates for the changes recommended during the study phase. Participants included diverse constituencies such as community agencies, advocates, politicians and funders. In addition, community development ensures a flexibility of approach which builds on the experience within the project and gives attention to the process as well as the product.

Using an action research framework

The action research framework was vital to successfully carrying out the project. However, it is necessary to consider what research is before specifying how action research is different.

Research is a process which begins with people asking questions, then setting out to answer them. They do this by systematically and rigorously collecting observations and imaginatively generating explanations for them. General research approaches include, for example, survey, evaluation, community study, and action research.

Action research is research that explicitly recognises its action component. That is, the idea that change inevitably results from the research process is acknowledged and consciously built into the basic design, so that we plan change, observe, reflect and act. Instead of the research ending with recommendations for action, this is simply the beginning (or part one) of the research process, which then goes on to implement that action, study it, feed back the results, and so on.

Action research is essentially participative research. Findings and new recommendations cannot be imposed but must be accepted by the subjects of the research. Hence the 'researched' must be involved at all stages of the research—they must see it as their research, as being in their interests, and as something they can affect so it works better for them. There is a need to involve people in the process of defining problems and the action required to resolve them.

Action research differs from traditional research in a variety of important ways, including the choice of the research problem, the goals of the research, the role of the researcher, and the process of the research. And while traditional research is primarily concerned with representing the interests of the sponsors, action research is more political because it is public and helps to explicitly define the interests of all participants. In such an atmosphere, researchers are more collaborators in action than analysts or consultants; they are involved in the general plan but cannot fully control the research; they integrate the results first into practice, then into theory; and they are concerned with direct application in the field, where results contribute to social improvements (Alary, p.243–245).

Developing a program for change

The program for change emerging out of the SPC's community-wide social research became the 'widely acceptable' change program within the metropolitan community. The community development focus allowed for widespread community ownership of the results. The recommended change program became the substance of funding proposals from community agencies as well as the agenda for change for community activists and representatives of mainstream and ethnospecific agencies coordinated through the Access Action Council. The change program has enormous implications for the possibilities for changing organisations, their relations, and funding systems within the community.

The development of a change program is in accord with Biklen's conception of action research that 'in addition to challenging conventions of who may do policy research, how policy research is to be done, and to what end, action research does not subscribe to the notion that research is or should be independent and neutral' (p.245). One important difference may be that traditional research is concerned with research about action, whereas action research may be seen as research for action.

Creating an imperative for changing organisations

The program encouraged organisational change toward multi-culturalism on the part of the mainstream or generalist agencies, which need to have a program for action, not simply pious intentions. The focus on organisational and inter-organisational change was vital, as the disadvantages faced by minorities are often seen as individual or group characteristics rather than institutional barriers residing in agencies.

For example, the prevailing belief is that ethnic populations do not receive services because they can't speak English, or because they do not understand the role of helping agencies or don't come for help to formal helping agencies (as they are said to prefer the help of family or friends). But few mainstream agencies and large societal institutions outside of government have seriously undergone any organisational change toward multiculturalism. Human services agencies need to implement planned and progressive change programs, giving attention to the change process, resistance to change, and a multiplicity of factors such as the pace of change, the degree of involvement by various constituencies, and making explicit the costs and benefits of change (Doyle & Rahi, 1990).

Using a structure for community action

Change strategies can be devised, based on different situations and using collaboration, persuasion and other means. However, first it is necessary to establish an organisation which can provide the structure for organised and coordinated community action. In Toronto, the organisational vehicle the community used to undertake change efforts was the Access Action Council, composed of individuals from both mainstream and ethnospecific agencies and organisations. The AAC became a useful forum for discussing concerns, for undertaking research and advocacy, and for providing educational opportunities such as workshops, conferences and forums. It involved itself in a whole range of issues, including race relations and policing, refugee matters, problems of the ethnic aged and minority youth concerns.

It is necessary to nominate or establish a community organisation as the vehicle to develop and maintain a community program that will pursue deliberate strategies for change. Change toward multi-culturalism will not serendipitously 'happen' but will be the result of some agencies changing voluntarily and other agencies being influenced (gently or otherwise) to 'become multicultural'. Community action is required to ensure access and equity within agencies and the services system, to demonstrate that multiculturalism is not simply a government contrivance but a reality in our societies. An organisational vehicle is needed to ensure coordinated and sustained community action for defining, designing, implementing and monitoring change in agencies, government and the community.

The development of organisations to control the research process is in keeping with concepts of participatory research which originated in the Third World as a response to inadequacies of so-called 'objective science' in identifying situations of urgent social and economic need. Some of the main characteristics of participatory research (PRIA:1985) are:

1   Control over the process of research jointly exercised by researchers and others involved; and the control over knowledge, outcomes and learning is not held by researchers.
2   Methodologies used attempt a praxis of theory and practice.
3   Empowerment of the relatively powerless as central to participatory research.
4   The research process strengthens or creates organisations of people so that social change in the interests of the 'have nots' is set in motion.

There seems no better way to leave our discussion of practice research than with the observation that organisation is required if practitioners are to genuinely assist in empowering the relatively powerless in the services system—the line workers or 'street bureaucrats' as well as service consumers or participants. One might look at the experience of the Brotherhood of St Laurence and its innovative work in Australia on the empowerment of the poor (Gilley, 1990; Weeks, 1988).

CONCLUSION

I have presented an example from Canada which demonstrates that research can be designed with a community development focus and can inform and reinforce the community action process for change within mainstream agencies to promote access and equity for members of cultural and racial minority groups.

The case example notes that improving access and equity will be complex and demanding. I have outlined a comprehensive approach to change, a program of change which addresses change within agencies, in relations among agencies, at the system level, and at the level of the society. Agencies will need to genuinely involve various stakeholders in change processes and develop a program, strategies, and a structure for directing the change process. Moreover, they will need to address both internal organisational change and change in the wider network or web of service organisations. In addition, a community-organisation vehicle is needed as a catalyst and focal point for organised efforts to improve access.

REFERENCES

Alary, Jacques (ed.) (1990) *Community Care and Participatory Research*, Nu-Age Editions, Montreal

Biklen, Douglas P., (1983) *Community Organizing: Theory and Practice*, Prentice-Hall, Englewood Cliffs

Department of the Prime Minister and Cabinet (1989) *National Agenda for a Multicultural Agenda*, Australian Government Publishing Service, Canberra, July

Doyle, Robert (1993), 'An evaluation of the Australian government's policy of access and equity in selected localities', *Journal of Health and Social Policy*, vol. 5, no. 2

Doyle, Robert and Rahi, Khan (1990) *Organization Change Toward Multiculturalism*, Access Action Council, Toronto

Doyle, Robert and Visano, Livy (1987a) *A Time for Action!, Volume 1 and A Program for Action, Volume 2: Access to Health and Social Services for Members of Diverse Cultural and Racial Groups*, Social Planning Council of Metropolitan Toronto, Toronto

Ethnicity and Aging (1988), *Report of a National Workshop on Ethnicity and Aging, 21–24 February*, Canadian Public Health Association, Ottawa

Foster, Chris and Kendig, Hal L. (eds.) (1987) *Who Pays $: Financing Services for Older People*, ANUTECH, Canberra

Gilley, Tim (1990) *Empowering Poor People*, Brotherhood of St Laurence, Melbourne

Jupp, J. (1992) *Access and Equity Evaluation Research*, Australian Government Printing Service, Canberra

Kahn, Alfred J. (1973) *Social Policy and Social Services*, Random House, New York

Liffman, Michael (1981) *Immigrant Welfare: A Research Perspective*, Social Welfare Research Centre, University of New South Wales, Sydney

Perlman, Robert (1975) *Consumers and Social Services*, John Wiley & Sons, New York

PRIA (1985), *Knowledge and Social Change: An Inquiry into Participatory Research in India*, Society for Participatory Research in Asia, New Delhi

Tator, Carol, (1990) 'Strategy for fostering participation and equity in the human services delivery system' in Robert Doyle and Khan Rahi, *Organization Change Toward Multiculturalism*, Access Action Council, Toronto

Weeks, Wendy (1988) 'De-professionalisation or a new approach to professionalisation?', *Australian Social Work*, vol. 41, no. 1

7   In doing you learn: Some reflections on practice research on an advocacy project
Bill Healy

This is a story about the 'doing' of a relatively large-scale research project which aimed to describe and better understand an innovative form of practice, advocacy in psychiatric services. It is not an account of the findings of that project but an attempt, through reflective analysis, to articulate some of my learning about the process of practice research. It is also an attempt to identify, as a consequence, how the notion of data, so sacred to researchers, can and ought to be more generously understood so as to incorporate the personal experiences, and their reflective meanings, that flow from actually undertaking the research.

This chapter emerges from a collaboration between myself, my co-investigator, Dr Patricia Moyniham of the Royal Melbourne Institute of Technology, and Ms Genevieve Goonan, a research assistant with the National Centre for Socio-Legal Studies at La Trobe University.

ESPOUSED METHOD

For me, the most powerful metaphor for this kind of research and related learning is that of a journey, so that:

> The researcher who searches for and discovers a research method is similar to a traveller who sets out on a journey with an anticipated itinerary; sometimes things go to plan and sometimes things change according to contingencies along the way. (Taylor, 1993, p.123)

Moreover, for me at least, this metaphorical journey became as important for the often unanticipated things that happened along the way as it did for the more formal and sought-after data which was accumulated through a variety of conventional methods. Thus that hoary old aphorism of Marshall McLuhan, 'The medium is the message', might be rephrased 'The doing is the message'. Or in more conventional terms, the attempt to do research may often be understood as an analogue of the very activities being investigated and thus reveals much about the subject of the research.

Much of the formal writing and teaching about research in social work draws explicitly and implicitly upon an espoused model of natural science. This has long been true of what might be termed 'basic research' within the discipline but is equally true of the more recently differentiated activity known as practice research (see Grinell, 1988). That is, we anticipate that:

1 The research process will proceed in a linear fashion, from problem specification through literature review, research questions, methodology, data gathering and analysis to the formulation of results and conclusions.
2 It will be relatively uncomplicated once under way in the sense that any problems that arises will be of a technical rather than a substantive nature.
3 Detachment is both desirable and possible.
4 Objectivity is crucial to maintaining a minimal level of scientific rigour and to the formulation of valid results.

A great deal of this understanding reflects a behaviourist set of assumptions which have long dominated discourse about and conventions within psychological and social research. Some values which are espoused as fundamental operative guidelines include detachment, objectivity and scientific rigour. One critic of this paradigm terms it the 'pseudoscientific approach' (Pieper, 1985, p.3). She continues:

> In the pseudoscientific utopia, all problems are 'empirical',
> measurable, quantifiable, operationalized, simplified, and resolvable.
> The ideal researcher is, in this utopia, objective, free of bias, removed
> from the clients or subjects being studied, and knowledgeable about
> inferential statistics, and the knowledge he or she seeks is 'grounded',
> nomothetic (lawlike), universal, and technological.

Moreover, pressure to follow this form of research paradigm comes from professional, organisational, academic, and funding bodies. In this case, our proposal was successful in attracting support from the Australian Research Council collaborative grants scheme, which is regarded as cautious, even unsympathetic, towards research designs which depart from the conventional 'scientific' approach. It is important to remember that there may be a complex politics at work, even in initial stages, which can be a minefield for the issue-focused practitioner who believes she or he is setting out simply to better understand some aspect of practice.

At the same time, we sought to develop an approach which was 'true' to the environment being studied and which, given our assumptions about the nature and complexity of the world of social and health services, required a substantial commitment to a variety of methodologies, especially qualitative but also quantitative. To return to the metaphor of the journey:

> Methods are like maps: They focus inquiry and lay out paths that, if followed, are supposed to lead to valid knowledge of how the world works. But like maps we consult in everyday life, they contain assumptions about what is important. Different maps make certain features of the terrain visible, and obscure others . . . Not objective pictures, maps are instead representations of reality that reflect the interests of the mapmaker, a point of view . . . Like research methods, maps are powerful tools for making statements about social life. Different ones connect us to realities we could not know without the map. (Riessman, 1994, p.xiii–xiv)

We set out on our journey with a variety of maps or methods: interviews, document and file searches, statistical analysis of databases, participation, observation and consultations. Overall we were guided by something like the five assumptions that Ruckdeschel identifies as the 'core elements' of the qualitative approach and of social work practice:

- People are essentially interpretative and symbol constructing.
- Knowledge is gained most directly by the process of participation and involvement.
- Reality is multilayered and multiperspectual
- Perception and behaviour are strongly influenced by the context in which they occur.
- Data gathering must involve the use of multiple sources and multiple methods.' (Ruckdeschel, 1985, p.18)

Thus, on the basis of these assumptions, we developed a mixed, though essentially qualitative, form of methodology. In so doing we had anticipated some, though not all, of the difficulties and *therefore* opportunities of reflective research practice. In consequence, this chapter tells the story of a research project which at first sight is a sad and sorry tale of frustration, many failures and some successes. The process has been the very antithesis of the idealised model— convoluted, intensely complicated, enmeshed in politics and driven by passion. As well it reveals that these experiences directly mirror the world of its investigations and that in consequence the findings of the project are based as much in the process of attempting to study the world as in the formal, explicit process of research. Reflecting upon our experiences of our work worlds is a legitimate means of exploring, understanding and therefore researching practice.

THE PROJECT

Policy and practice contexts

Psychiatric or mental health services are one of the 'Cinderella' areas of social policy, long neglected by and hidden from public political debate. As a result, for most of the past 200 years they have been typified more by custodial and control agendas, usually mediated through the concerns of powerful vested interests, than by treatment or rehabilitation purposes. To become a psychiatric patient, especially an involuntary one in the public system, has meant the loss of autonomy, freedom, dignity and basic civil and human rights. In consequence, the receipt of services has resulted in patients becoming isolated, marginalised, poor and powerless. During more than 25 years working in the mental health field I have been constantly moved to feelings of frustration and anger by the plight of patients. Often it has seemed that the constant cycles of scandal, investigation and reform have led only to more of the same. For me, and indeed for many other practitioners, this has resulted in a ceaseless search for more fundamental and incisive ideas about how to improve the basic conditions of life in psychiatric institutions. At various times I have seen periodical rises in optimism as the promises of innovations and reforms like psychotropic drugs, community mental health programs, new social and psychological therapies, policy and legislative reforms and managerial interventions are presented as panaceas for the system. And yet, despite many and sometimes significant improvements, the world of psychiatric services somehow seems to maintain its fundamental ways of doing business. Not surprisingly, then, I, like many others, have come increasingly to believe that fundamental reform will most likely require inputs of ideas and practices from outside the relatively insulated world of psychiatry. I came to develop this project as a research inquiry about the conditions of everyday life in psychiatric institutions, their meanings in relation to basic legal, civil and human rights, and the potential remedies that might exist in the crossover between the worlds of law and psychiatry.

At the same time I was also driven by a long-held belief that an essential beginning point for any study of mental health services is a recognition that the history of the field serves to illuminate contemporary policy and practice. This is no more apparent than in the present case, where I am attempting to research the relationships between psychiatry, rights and advocacy. In the first place there has been for almost 200 years a constant tension between the two discourses, law and psychiatry, within which this present study is located. In the second place there has been a substantial critique of psychiatry emanating from the social sciences since at least the 1950s. Beginning with Goffman and his seminal studies of the often harsh realities of institutional life, down through the contributions of Laing, Szasz, Scheff and Foucault to the present, with writers like Scull, there has been an almost unceasing flow of criticism of a simplistic 'progressive' view of the benefits of psychiatric services and the related charge that as much damage as good is done to thousands of people by the intervention of mental health services into their lives. In more recent times, at least within Australia, there has also been a more particularly empirical and less theoretical approach exemplified in the various royal commissions and commissions of inquiry, and in the report of the Human Rights and Equal Rights Commission (known as the Burdekin Report), which have revealed a sorry state of affairs in relation to abuses of human rights and the inadequacies of remedial processes.

Not surprisingly, then, governments, both in Australia and around the world, have been giving increasing emphasis to the pivotal role of rights protection and related activities like advocacy in the achievement of policy and program integrity in the whole range of human services. In this context the adoption by the United Nations in December 1991 of the 'Principles for the protection of persons with mental illness and for the improvement of mental health care' represents a significant and long overdue internationally agreed-upon set of guidelines in the area of psychiatric services. These principles and protections give emphasis to, among other things, the need for clear criteria for involuntary detention; the placing of restrictions on the use of the more invasive forms of treatment; the requirement, where possible, of obtaining informed consent; the mandating of reviews and appeals and, of particular interest to this study, the establishing of 'a right to representation, advocacy and procedural fairness' (Zifcak, 1994, p.9).

It was against this backdrop that in April 1992 the first national mental health policy was launched by the health ministers of the Commonwealth, states and territories of Australia. The policy emphasises that rights are central to the delivery of services to the mentally ill:

> People with mental health problems and mental disorders are
> particularly vulnerable to infringement of their civil and human rights

and to discrimination. The national mental health policy seeks to establish a framework for the protection of their rights and civil liberties as set down in the Australian health ministers' mental health statement of rights and responsibilities and in the United Nations Resolution on the protection of rights of people with a mental illness. (Australian Health Ministers, 1992)

It was in these contexts that the Victorian health minister announced in April 1991 a series of reforms for state psychiatric services which included the development of an advocacy program specifically for psychiatric services and to operate under the auspices of the established Office of the Public Advocate. This program was implemented under the name 'Advocates in Psychiatric Services' and represented the belief that advocacy is a means of protecting against and remedying rights violations within psychiatric institutions. Now there was a rights-oriented advocacy program that provided an opportunity for the kind of research I had long been seeking. And so, after much discussion, negotiation and many hiccups we formed a collaborative relationship with the Office of the Public Advocate and made a submission to the Australian Research Council. It was this body's funding criteria, that they support 'basic research' and not evaluation (the interest of our collaborator), that set our project on its present course.

Our key research question became: Can the advocacy process work to guarantee rights when it is located in psychiatric services? Additional specific questions were:

1   What is successful advocacy in the psychiatric setting?
2   What outcomes are being sought for consumers?
3   How can they be assessed in theory and practice?
4   Does advocacy meet its own criteria of success? Under what conditions, with whom and where?
5   What is the nature of the advocacy program that is being introduced into psychiatric services?
6   What if any barriers can be identified in respect to: (i) implementation and (ii) successful operation of the advocacy process?
7   How could the program operate so that it is more successful?
8   Are the outcomes of the process conditional upon social system characteristics of the consumer such as age, gender, ethnicity, length of stay, status of admission and/or the institutional context in which they are receiving treatment?

The next stage, project design, evolved, as with everything else, through the combined influences of the researchers' professional identities (social work and sociology), the funding-body criteria ('respectable' social science methodologies), the realities of the various involved agencies (Office of the Public Advocate, Psychiatric Services) and the capacities, interests and motivations of the potential participants (patients, advocates, psychiatric workers). What emerged was a design that focused on a range of sites for data collection and which proposed the utilisation of multiple methods. Thus, for instance, we planned to access the advocacy program's database and subject it to quantitative analyses; search files; interview key informants involved in the policy and program development as well as those most involved in delivering, receiving and witnessing the program. In so doing we proposed using a variety of qualitative measures and forms of analysis such as focused interviews, content analysis and participant observation.

Implementing the research

Writing the grant application often seems to me to be the hardest part of a project. In this instance, if I thought that to be the case I was in for some terrible shocks for within a very short time after receiving the news of our success in obtaining ARC funds a conservative state government was elected in Victoria. While it is arguably unwise, if not slightly neurotic, to personalise changes in the political system, I could be, I think, forgiven for doing so in this instance. The change of government was from one that had brought into being the legislative, policy and program reforms in psychiatric services which, among other things, enhanced the rights of patients, to one that was committed to both fundamental philosophical change and savage expenditure cuts antagonistic to that reform. One important and almost immediate outcome was a drastic and turbulent destabilisation of public-sector policy and management.

At first we could not even arrange a meeting with our collaborator, the Office of the Public Advocate. Letters were unanswered and phone calls not returned for some months. Finally a meeting was arranged at which we were informed that the project could not proceed because the office's budget was to be cut by at least 10 per cent. For us this was a strange explanation, as the basis of our collaboration had been that the ARC funds were pegged to a specified amount of 'in kind' funding from the office, and as such should not be affected by budget cuts. When we reiterated that no money was being sought from the office, we were told that the project would place too many demands on staff already overburdened by the budget cuts. We proposed, in the absence of any better idea, that there be no rush to make a final decision and that we would amend our protocols so as to place minimal additional stress on the advocates. Some time later, again after a period of no response to our letters, proposals or phone calls, I was summoned to the office, not, as it turned out, for an anticipated meeting, but to be handed a personal letter from the public advocate which formally terminated our collaborative research agreement. The next day he left on extended leave and was absent from the country for some two months. We, the research team, decided to file this letter under 'pending' and to reopen negotiations with his deputy, the acting public advocate. Finally we broke through and, almost one year late, were able to begin the project proper. The breakthrough, it emerged later, owed less to the brilliance of our proposal than it did to a reinterpretation of the strategic interests of the office. With the temporary change of leadership came the realisation that while research can expose and embarrass, it can also serve to bolster and even justify activities. In other words, politics was still at work, only now our project had become to symbolise possibility rather than threat.

Once again my jubilation at a victory over the 'forces of darkness' was short lived, for now we had to shepherd our proposal through five separate psychiatric services research and ethics committees which, at least in our experience, are often, though not always, driven by a bizarre mix of professional, academic and organisational politics. Moreover, each one seemed almost obliged to require that its own version of either research protocols or ethics procedures be followed without necessary reference to other committees. All of which leads, to return to the metaphor of the journey, to endless meandering down byways and around roundabouts, with frequent lengthy stops in laybys and a recurring nightmare that the research would never commence but be condemned to a perpetual life of pointless attempts at self-justification. What could we say, for instance, to the comment of a senior clinician/researcher on one such committee that 'I don't like qualitative research', especially when he was one of a group with almost unfettered power to say yea or nay to our project?

Having successfully worked our way through these committees, we had to start negotiating our way into each institution, into their particular program areas (e.g. acute, rehabilitation, psychogeriatric) and finally, one by one, into specific wards to arrange interviews with patients and staff about their views and experiences of rights and advocacy in a psychiatric setting. At each step we received guarded verbal expressions of cooperation followed by, in most instances, a series of delays and altered or failed arrangements and appointments—all pervaded by what has felt like passive resistance. On several occasions, for instance, one of the researchers, on arriving at a ward at a prearranged time, was greeted with the information that 'There are hardly any patients around as they have gone out

on an excursion'. Or, again, 'What was it you wanted to do?' At
the very least we seem to have discovered that research, and perhaps
research about rights and advocacy, has a low priority within mental
health services, not least because the demands of everyday work seem
to leave little time for thinking about and reflecting on something
perceived as less than immediately urgent.

In the midst of all this the new state government proceeded to
cut, slash and burn its way through the health and community
services sector. Frustration ran high in the Office of the Public
Advocate, to such an extent that even before we could commence
field work all of the original group of six psychiatric advocates had
resigned, to be replaced by only *two* new advocates who still faced
the same workload that had been experienced as too much by their
six predecessors. Morale among state employees seemed to be plum-
meting, and the secretary of the Health and Community Services
department publicly characterised advocacy services as 'all piss and
wind'. By the middle of our first year of research, the government
decided to de-fund the Advocates in Psychiatric Services program
partly because the original funding period was coming to an end but
also because, the minister asserted, the success of his government's
reforms of the psychiatric system meant that such services were now
redundant!

Despite these difficulties, and thanks in part to the efforts of
cooperative staff, the project has maintained its momentum and at
the time of writing we have almost completed our field-work interviews, document and file searches and interviews with most of the
key 'players' in the policy processes.

AN EMERGENT THEORY AND METHOD OF REFLECTIVE
RESEARCH

A sad and sorry tale? Yes, and one that has frequently tested my
resolve not only to complete the project but also to plan any further
practice research. Yet slowly but surely, as we struggled through the
seemingly never-ending morass of delays, sidetracks and frustration,
I began to see that what we were experiencing was in many startling
ways parallel, or analogous to, what the Advocacy in Psychiatric
Services program and its workers had gone through as they developed
their ideas, attempted to implement their program, negotiated their
way through access to the institutions and attempted to deliver their
services to their prospective clientele. Indeed, interviews with several
of the original advocates later confirmed that they had experienced
many of the same frustrations, delays and sidetracks that we encountered. Very rarely, for instance, did anyone in the psychiatric system

actually voice opposition to their program. Rather, like us, they encountered opaque forms of opposition, rather like being stuck in a bowl of porridge or similarly gluggy material. You know, to use another analogy, that you are swimming in the dark. That is, as you attempt to work your way through the morass it feels as if you are getting nowhere, especially as you can't readily see or identify the bits of blockage that slow you down. Eventually, though, you reach the end and can begin the task of deciphering the shapes and colours of the various obstacles that you have bumped into along the way.

Our experiences of attempting to launch and implement the research taught us much about the nature and meaning of the phenomena under study. Specifically we learnt that:

- no piece or form of practice can be understood without a detailed, critical and reflective analysis of its multiple contexts of operation. Each step of our journey bears witness to this claim and illuminates the basic question of the relationships between advocacy, rights and psychiatric settings needing to be approached as having different meanings within various organisations, political agendas, historical trends and intellectual traditions;
- organisational processes bear directly and powerfully on opportunities for practice in ways which have little or no bearing on its intrinsic meaning or value. Inevitably other people do not share your sense of enthusiasm or urgency, being naturally preoccupied with the more immediate issues of their everyday work;
- interprofessional and ideological rivalries can and do distort opportunities for research and practice and require vigilance and perseverance if they are to be overcome. There are, for instance, structural reasons why psychiatric staff will be suspicious of advocates and vice versa. Moreover, researchers will be treated with a fair degree of scepticism, and perhaps with good reason, about their intentions, capacities and true loyalties;
- institutions are hostile, albeit in a passive-resistant way, to incursions from the outside, especially, as was the case here, where there are inherent tensions, even contradictions, between the two. Therefore one answer to the question of whether advocacy can deliver on rights is that this depends on its (the program's) ability to cross the organisational divide;
- these tensions are further exacerbated by the current climate of massive external changes in policy, politics, organisational structures, industrial struggles and levels of funding that bear down on all staff. Being a practitioner has probably never been more difficult. Under these circumstances, who needs an apparently friendly though probably meddlesome researcher hanging around asking distracting questions?

- offers of cooperation from institutional staff are sometimes/often a cover for obstructionism or are delaying tactics as they struggle to find ways to get rid of you or hope that you will lose patience and simply go away;
- the local culture of a unit of an organisation may often be more preoccupied with self-defined issues of survival than anything else and, understandably, may be relatively uninterested in both the content and purpose of any research project. Not surprisingly, then, notions of patients' rights and advocacy, as pursued in this project, turn out to be at least of very low priority in the life of institutions or at worst become no more than a focus for hostility from staff who feel unappreciated and devalued by their superiors;
- program implementation, at the point of service delivery, is as much about the politics of institutional life and about the relationship between the centre and the periphery of the organisation as it is about the coming into life of a worthy and compelling idea;
- the external, political world of human services is a potent factor in determining which ideas get up and which don't—it is arguable in this instance that while a tired old government wished to be seen to be doing something right, a 'newish' government and its eager bureaucracy, hell bent on reform, do not want to be reminded of still-unsolved problems in one of their principal areas of service.

In terms of insights about method, I have learnt or had reinforced that:

- data collection doesn't begin and end with the formal phases of the research but is an integral part of the whole process of inquiry. The experience of collecting data is also to be understood as data, and indeed may, as in this instance, be of considerable significance in understanding the reception of a practice innovation;
- in particular, the reactions and responses of individuals and institutions to proposing and undertaking research into practice reveal a great deal about how they already understand and evaluate it. Very often actions do speak louder than words, a reality often obscured by policy and 'marketing' rhetoric;
- delays, obstructions and frustration ought not be thought of merely as problematic for an individual researcher but should be used to gain insight and understanding into institutional responses to the practice under investigation. Such events are, in this sense, better able to be appreciated and tolerated as opportunities for learning than as obstacles to doing the research;

- practice research seems to place a premium on the need for multiple methods to accommodate the complexity of the social world. Such a stance also, of course, assumes that the same is true for any attempts to advance practice and in consequence makes critical, reflective, context-related and strategic thinking mandatory in developing practice and related research.

The research 'journey' described here has obviously often been a difficult one for me. At the same time it has been a rewarding experience ultimately satisfying and rich in learning. If I were to start it over again I would undoubtedly do many things differently. In particular, I would better anticipate oppositions and blockages. The research process will continue to be replete with difficulties but I now know these are tolerable, even desirable, because of their capacity to provide rich data and insights into the issues under investigation. Stevens, writing of her experiences in choosing an appropriate method for her postgraduate research, captures the essential threatening and rewarding qualities of reflective practice and inquiry:

> The selection of an appropriate research methodology and the need to subsequently justify that selection can be likened to jumping from an aeroplane and discovering that your parachute will not open. Nothing is certain, everything is problematic. You resolve one dilemma only to have it replaced by several more. Questions regarding subjectivity, ownership of data, how to obtain data without compromising the people being researched, how to remain objective enough to distinguish between people's reasoned objections and false consciousness, how to decide if in fact it is not you that is suffering from 'ideological block'; all remain largely unanswered. In the end the best way perhaps is to learn by your mistakes. (Stevens, 1993, p.167)

REFERENCES

Australian Health Ministers (1992) *National Mental Health Policy*, Australian Government Publishing Service, Canberra

Colquhoun, D. and Kellehear, A. (eds) (1993) *Health Research in Practice: Political, Ethical and Methodological Issues*, Chapman & Hall, London

Grinnell, R. (ed) (1988) *Social Work Research and Evaluation*, F.E. Peacock, Itasca

Pieper, M. (1985) 'The future of social work research', *Social Work Research and Abstracts*, vol. 21, no. 4

Riessman, C. (1994) *Qualitative Studies in Social Work Research*, Sage, Thousand Oaks, California

Ruckdeschel, R. (1985) 'Qualitative research as a perspective', *Social Work Research and Abstracts*, vol. 21, no. 2

Stevens, L. (1993) 'Reflexivity: Recognising subjectivity in research', in
    Colquhoun, D. & Kellehear, A. (eds) *Health Research in Practice*,
    Chapman and Hall, London
Taylor, B. (1993) 'Phenomenological method in nursing: Theory vs. reality',
    in Colquhoun, D. and Kellehear, A. (eds) *Health Research in Practice*,
    Chapman & Hall, London
Zifcak, S. (1994) 'The United Nations principles for the protection of people
    with mental illness and the Victorian mental health system', in National
    Centre for Socio-Legal Studies, *Human Rights, the Law and Psychiatry*,
    La Trobe University, Bundoora

Part III

Choosing research design and methodology

8

Finding a methodology to meet the needs of research: Moving towards a participatory approach

Carmel Laragy

I started upon this path of seeking an appropriate research methodology when I commenced my PhD studies. As I write this I am nearing the end of the data collection and have made the necessary decisions about the research design. It has been a time of learning and reflection and changing ideas along the way as I worked to meet my research aims. My main aim has been to conduct staff development programs for social workers within their agencies and evaluate whether these were useful to participants. This interest in working with groups of social workers at their workplace stemmed from a growing understanding that their relationship with their employing agency was critical to the way they worked and to the profession's survival.

BACKGROUND

My experience as a social work educator at university, where I taught skills programs and supervised placements, was the background to my interest in how social workers cope in the workplace. From teaching undergraduates I moved to running private training programs for qualified workers, who came from various sites. This was challenging and exciting because each program was created in response to the issues participants brought with them. It also gave me the opportunity to use action methods, which I had been training in over a number of years. This is a methodology stemming from psychodrama that was created by Jacob Moreno. Moreno trained as a psychiatrist in Vienna in 1917 and later moved to the United States, where he developed group training and counselling methods over many years (Williams, 1989, p.9).

I first went to a psychodrama workshop for my own personal development and to review issues I was working on at the time. I found the strength of action methods was the way it set out personal and social relationships in a concrete and manageable form. This was a revelation. It gave me an opportunity to explore my past, observe my way of dealing with problems, and try out new ways of dealing with situations. I also liked the fact that no-one was telling me what I should or shouldn't do and imposing solutions on me. Sometimes my own responses were mirrored back to me by others; at times the leader asked members of the group to enact how they would deal with a situation. Finally it was up to me to find, in what had been presented, answers I felt were adequate and satisfactory to me. I found that this process of discovery in a safe and protected environment was enormously helpful when I went out to the real world because I had a wider repertoire of responses to draw upon.

After my initial introduction to psychodrama I began training to bring this methodology into my professional work, as I could see it would have direct application to teaching social work skills. In educational settings it is referred to as action methods, is restricted to issues relevant to the professional setting and does not intrude into personal background. But its usefulness is still its ability to help people find new ways of dealing with practical situations. It was exciting and rewarding to bring this method to social work training and my evaluation of the program indicated that participants also found it stimulating and useful.

IN THE BEGINNING

I began my research project with two formal goals. The first was to explore the relationship between social workers and other staff members in their employing organisations. This was to be achieved through observing the issues people raised in the training program as well as through interviews with participants and other staff in the organisation. The second goal was to evaluate my own work and see whether the type of program I was offering was valuable to the workers. I believe all professionals have to be able to establish the value of their work in this competitive world. Therefore I wanted a thorough evaluation to show to others what I was doing as well as for my own satisfaction.

When I started thinking about my research I had a collection of ideas which were all jumbled together. It took me some time to realise that some were contradictory. I wanted to run training programs for social workers in their place of employment with the participants determining the agenda and being full and active participants in the process. But I also wanted a structured program with a predetermined agenda that I could repeat in different settings. This would have clear aims decided in advance so I could use the same criteria to evaluate each program. I wanted to test whether the programs were effective or not. The underlying philosophies of these two approaches are quite different and it took me some time to really understand this, even though I had studied it at a theoretical level. I will look at the stages I went through in coming to this discovery.

After working with social workers who had come together from various locations, I was keen to work with social workers within one agency for a number of reasons. Previously I had found that participants came to training, received stimulation and new ideas and reported an improvement in their abilities back at work. I wanted to investigate in more detail whether their new ideas really were useful to them in their workplace and also whether they were appreciated by others within their organisations. I was aware that the social work role is intimately tied to the organisational context in which it occurs. As Jones and May (1992, p.5) point out, almost all social workers are dependent on their employing organisations for their legitimacy and survival. A major focus of my research was to explore the relationship between social workers and their employing organisations.

I thought it was important that participants, as adult learners, set their own goals and have considerable influence on the agenda of the program. I realised that, as the facilitator, my personality and range of skills would restrict what we could do, but within my limitations I wanted them to be working towards goals they determined. My experience in psychodrama and my reading of the literature had convinced me that the most effective learning takes place when people have the opportunity to work on issues relevant to them. It also led me to understand that the world is not made up of a number of facts which are obvious to everyone who looks at them. Any one situation can be viewed from many different angles and what people see is dependent upon the knowledge and frame of reference they bring with them. Two people observing an incident can give two honest but totally different accounts of what has happened because they perceive different elements contained within it.

This interest in the way people see the world differently led me to George Kelly's 'personal construct theory' (1955). Kelly described how everybody views the world differently and how our experience and the sense we make of it shapes the way we anticipate and

interpret events. Kelly's followers have developed statistical procedures for identifying the way a person views a situation and I decided
I would incorporate these into my methodology as one means of
evaluating the effectiveness of my programs. I will give details a little
later.

RESEARCH APPROACHES

When I looked at what I wanted to do and read literature on the
philosophical basis of research, I found a position where my work
fitted and where I felt very comfortable. It went under different labels
in different books and they were usually long and complicated, like
'ethnographic-inductive' (Kellehear, 1993, p.36), and 'dialectic epistemology' (Zuber-Skerritt, 1992, p.35). These terms described a way
of learning whereby the researcher goes into a situation with an open
mind and tries to describe it from the other person's point of view.
The real world is not considered a fixed objective reality but is made
up of the ways people see it. Conclusions and theories to describe
relationships between people are drawn from the study and are not
formulated before the research begins. In this perspective, learning
is always viewed as an active process in which the facilitator and
the learner reflect on new knowledge and fit this together with past
understandings.

This approach to learning and research stands in contrast to a
'positivist' or 'traditional epistemology' one. A positivist approach
begins with a theory to be tested and assumes there is an objective
reality out there waiting to be discovered. It considers that knowledge
about the real world can be accumulated by proving or disproving
facts through measuring and testing. In this approach to learning the
teacher is considered to be the holder of knowledge which is passed
on to a less-informed pupil. However, this approach is thought by
many to be best suited to gathering information about the physical
world and less suited to learning about complex interpersonal situations.

In the beginning I assumed I would use a positivist model. My
plan was to develop the best possible training program I could and
then conduct this, without change, in three different settings. I hoped
to standardise the procedure and so reduce the number of variables.
My early training in mathematics and science had left me valuing
an ordered, positivist approach in which I could control as many
variables as possible and later draw clear conclusions by proving or
disproving an hypothesis. This model has been prized in Western
society since the late 1800s, when Comte first introduced it with the
aim of building knowledge in an orderly and systematic fashion

(Schon, 1983, p.32). I certainly had inherited a good dose of this philosophy and began by assuming I would undertake my research in this systematic way.

As I began to plan what I would actually do, it slowly dawned on me that I could not have a set program while also giving control to participants. There was a fundamental contradiction in planning to explore the experiences of participants in an open, unstructured manner while also wanting to repeat the same course with different people. I had expected that my hypothesis would be something like, 'This program is useful to participants'. However, this raised the question, 'What does useful mean?' I was back again to individual interpretation. I did not have a clear hypothesis I was testing. I was really going into the workplace to explore what issues were important to workers while using my own background and experience to discover with them the best ways of seeking adequate solutions.

In other ways, too, I was not in step with the positivist way of viewing things. I wanted to interview a range of people within the organisations to ask about their expectations of social work and about their current working relationship. I fully accepted that different people have their own perception and expectations and to me the important issue seemed to be how these all fit together. I did not consider it helpful to try to determine who was absolutely right or wrong when it came to examining values, expectations and emotions. This took me out of the positivist camp, which tends to look for absolutes. Another problem I had fitting into a positivist framework was that it would not allow me to learn from my experiences in one setting and adapt my program accordingly. Once I had a set model, this would be fixed and unresponsive to changing conditions and opportunities. The more I considered the practicalities of my work, the more I realised I was not a positivist. I wanted to be flexible and responsive to changing environments and I needed a model that would allow me to be so.

ACTION RESEARCH

To take full advantage of the information available to me, I turned to an action research model. This step was prompted by suggestions from my supervisor. The great benefit of action research was that it allowed me to incorporate knowledge as I progressed so I could change procedures in later settings to meet the different demands. By adopting this model instead of trying to be more positivist, I removed the contradictions I was struggling with. It is essential that there be congruence of purpose and methodology within one piece of research and I was pleased to find I had achieved this with action research. The decision to move to an action research model was a very easy and natural one when I discovered that it fitted in so well with the teaching method I was using and with the evaluation using personal construct theory.

Robin McTaggart (1991) gives an excellent and concise outline of action research. He mentions that the approach was developed by social psychologist Kurt Lewin in the 1940s and 1950s. Lewin described action research in theoretical terms as a series of spiral steps composed of planning, acting, observing and evaluating. These steps are repeated over and over within one piece of research, with participants playing a large part in determining future directions. It was intended that groups of people work together to review their situation with the intention of improving conditions for themselves. This implies that change comes from within the group and that solutions are not imposed from outside.

Lewin did not prescribe a rigid set of procedures for action research. This leaves room for debate among present-day researchers as to what really defines this approach. When I became seriously interested in adopting action research as my guiding framework, I was concerned that I might not have filled all its requirements. McTaggart outlined his definition of action research quite tightly and he stipulated that participants have to be part of a feedback loop wherein they are consulted before a further round of action is undertaken with them. I had concerns that I might not meet his criteria, as I did not plan to return to the same group of people to implement changes in a later round of interaction. My plan was to work with one group, evaluate the program with them, then move onto the next group. I contacted Robin McTaggart at Deakin University in Geelong and he kindly invited me to go and see him. It was very satisfying for me when he accepted my proposed research within the boundaries of action research.

The action research model not only dealt with the issue of my wanting to change my methodology as I proceeded but turned this difficulty into a positive attribute. As long as there were good reasons for wanting to change, the model encouraged me to be responsive and to change for the next stage. Action research also dealt with my dilemma of how to involve participants in deciding their own goals and the means of achieving them. Again, this became a reason for choosing action research because my goals and the model's requirements coincided.

It had occurred to me that I was attracted to methodologies that were phenomenological—that is, they attempted to see the world through the eyes of other people. Kelly's personal construct theory is entirely based on this, while action research and action methods teaching derived from psychodrama are very much user orientated and controlled. I felt there was a congruence between the methods I was planning to use in the study and I mentioned this to McTaggart. I was surprised and delighted when he told me that the origins of the three methodologies had common connections. He referred me to a chapter by Altrichter and Gstettner in a book he is currently editing in which they assert that Moreno, the founder of psychodrama, had a significant influence on Lewin and the development of action research. This connected the beginnings of all three methods, as I had already established that Kelly and Moreno had some cross-fertilisation in the development of their ideas (Stewart & Barry, 1991, p.121).

RESEARCH DESIGN

Having mentioned some of the issues I struggled with, I would like to explain what I actually did. My goals of exploring the relationship between social workers and others in their organisations and evaluating my own programs led me to a design which became quite complicated. One aspect was using my own impressions and reactions as a legitimate form of information in addition to the more statistically based measures. I was continually reflecting and writing a log of my impressions and emotional reactions. This was one way of gauging the atmosphere and tensions which existed for social workers.

By using different types of data I hoped to gain a picture of the situation from different angles. The literature encouraged this approach and spoke of its increasing the validity of the research if the results were complementary. If the results ended up contradicting each other, then I would have a problem, or at least I would be forced to look at issues I had previously ignored. One concern I did have with the design I chose was the volume of data I was gathering. In retrospect I could have made it simpler, had less data and still produced a respectable thesis. But my design grew in response to the opportunities that presented and I chose to take advantage of these.

When I negotiated to conduct my first training program I was still intending to use a strict positivist approach. The first setting was not intended to be part of my formal study but rather a trial run to help me 'find my feet' working in an organisational setting, which I hadn't done before. I also used it to test which of my ideas on evaluation would be acceptable. I consulted with group members and their senior social worker about evaluation and together we designed a procedure acceptable to everyone. I was nearing the completion of this program when I spoke to McTaggart and decided to use the action research framework. I was well aware that the input from the

people in this first organisation was shaping my thinking and assisting me in formulating my research structure. I was delighted to adopt
the action research framework because it meant I could recognise
this in my formal study. Also, much to my supervisor's relief, it meant
I was propelled a long way along with my research rather than being
at a preliminary stage.

With the blessing of action research, the research design changed
slightly from one setting to the next but still retained a general
pattern which was repeated in three settings. First, a group training
program was offered free of charge to welfare organisations employing social workers. Some organisations were contacted directly by
my supervisor and a general announcement was also made at a social
work training day for social work supervisors. Throughout this
recruiting process there were three false starts when initial negotiations began but it became clear to one side or the other that it was
not appropriate.

The first program to be conducted was at a federal government
agency, where I negotiated with the senior social worker to conduct
an eight-session program for Class 2 workers. Sessions took place
weekly or fortnightly and lasted about two hours. These staff were
front-line workers who worked directly with clients as well as having
supervisory responsibility for Class 1 workers. I spoke at a staff
meeting, offering an eight-session program whose agenda we would
design together. I suggested we might use case discussions, literature
reviews and action methods as possible ways of working. About a
dozen workers attended the meeting and six took up the offer. At
first I sensed some wariness from the group members; in later
discussions with them I learned this was because of fears that they
might be exposed before their peers and the information used to
their disadvantage. Also, action methods were new to them and, I
think, added to their concerns about exposure.

I asked their permission to conduct three different types of
research while I was with them. I asked if they would be willing to
write down their personal goals before coming to the program and
rate on a scale of 1 to 10 how they thought they were performing
in each area. I said they would be asked to repeat this at the end
of the program. Because I was keen to have some external evaluation
of the impact of the program, I asked if the senior social worker
could provide her estimate of change. I had discussed this with her
and she had suggested she write down the goals she hoped the
workers would achieve in the program. She suggested giving a before
and after rating for each individual and said she would discuss this
with each staff member at the conclusion of the program. Permission
was given for both these methods of evaluation, but a third request
was initially denied. I asked to interview managers within the

organisation to seek their views on the role of social work and what it offered the organisation. I was not looking for any individual evaluation. Only after the staff gained confidence in me some weeks into the program did they give permission for me to interview management.

In summary, at the end of the program I had before-and-after ratings on goals participants set for themselves and on goals the senior social worker had set which reflected her expectations for her staff. A Wilcoxon signed-rank test was used to assess whether there were any significant differences (Daniel, 1990, p.150). I also had taped interviews I conducted with participants at the conclusion of the program and with their managers. I transcribed and analysed this material, noting the themes which were presented. As I wanted to assess which aspects of my training program were helpful or otherwise to participants I used personal construct theory grids. By identifying the different components of the course, such as case discussion, literature reviews, the action work and so on, I was able to use a program called G-Pack (Bell, 1987) to assess which aspects of the program were influential.

The broad thrust of this procedure was repeated in two other agencies but with adjustments. Some I initiated after reviewing my methodology and some were forced upon me by the circumstances I met at the agencies. The second agency was a large public hospital and the group comprised senior social work staff at Class 2 and above. The focus of the program was on supervision, as they were having problems designing and implementing a workable supervision policy.

I changed my research design in a number of ways. First, I included taped interviews with participants before as well as after the program. Second, in addition to each person's individual goals I drew up a list of eight goals that I asked everyone to rate. I based these on the goals listed at the first agency, such as, 'Wanting more theoretical information' and 'Gaining confidence in my professional role'. I changed these slightly to direct them to the topic of supervision. Having a common set of goals for everyone gave me the opportunity to statistically analyse the whole group to see which areas were changing. This was in addition to each person's individual goals, which varied in number and scope. Finally, I asked this group if it was possible to get some external assessment of change in the way I had used the senior social worker previously. As all the senior social work staff were in the group, this would have meant asking hospital managers or members of other disciplines. This was considered practically and politically out of the question and was not pursued. Initially I was also refused permission to interview hospital managers, doctors and nurses about their expectations of social work. But as with the first group, when staff became reassured after working with me for some weeks, permission was granted and interviews proceeded with no difficulty. Information from interviews was always given back to the social work group.

Having members in the group from different hierarchical levels changed the dynamics considerably and also made me more aware of the difficulties facing senior staff at a time when social work is under considerable threat. I concluded that it is essential for social work to reach out to its employing agency, pursue a positive relationship and promote its contribution. An interest in social work becoming more entrepreneurial led me to my third group, which was working in this way. Again I was in a federal government agency, but this time with senior social work advisers who worked in middle management and acted as consultants to field staff. My procedures remained virtually the same but one difference was the goals I provided. I waited until I had interviewed group members and obtained their individual goals before compiling a summation of these and then presenting them to everyone for rating. Their interests and concerns seemed so different from those of front-line workers that I could not predict what their goals would be. All goals were rated before and after the program. I did not ask to obtain any external assessment of change but I did interview a wide range of staff members regarding their views of social work. These included senior management, peers in other disciplines and staff receiving the consulting services. Basically I was trying to obtain a perspective on social work from many different positions. I liken it to taking photographs of a scene from different angles.

WHAT TO DO WITH ALL THE INFORMATION

Having gathered all this information, I faced quite a challenge in condensing it so the important themes could be separated from the sea of detail. I found the hard statistical information the easiest to deal with, even though I still had to interpret the results in the light of all the other information. As I moved into the qualitative material open to interpretation, it became more difficult to justify why I was selecting and interpreting material in a certain way. The analysis of the group program using personal construct theory grids had its difficulties because the information is only suggestive of possible relationships and I was left feeling a little uncertain as to how reliable it all was. The biggest challenge was the analysis of the interviews. I selected themes from the different categories of people I interviewed, that is the front-line social workers, middle-management social workers, senior agency managers, participants' colleagues and subordinates. The themes were based on the content of the interviews and also upon my knowledge gained from all my interactions and reflections.

The usefulness of employing the different measures was that it gave different perspectives. The non-positivist approach to research that I adopted along the way supported the idea that no one method of collecting data would give a perfect picture of reality. They all contributed in their own way. No doubt I could have built up an adequate picture with less information, but I feel the different dimensions added a richness of their own.

When I look back over the research process I realise I have changed in a number of ways and my research reflects these changes. I began by looking for a neat, precise design that would have a conclusive outcome. This fitted in with the part of me which wanted to believe in an absolute reality. However, this approach conflicted with my desire to give control to participants and let them show what they believed the main issues to be. I had to let go of my desire for absolute answers and adjust to viewing the world as a collection of different perspectives. One of the most important lessons I learnt, or had to relearn, was the importance of review and reflection. My design evolved after talking to others, incorporating new ideas and reflecting on each stage before planning for the next. If by some magic I were starting over again I would probably keep the broad framework that I used but have a clearer focus on my aim to investigate the social workers' relationship with their employing organisation. Somehow I would keep my data collection simpler, although I am not sure what I would be prepared to eliminate. It has been a challenging and fascinating process, with times of tedium and anxiety. Certainly I have learnt much about social work and the huge challenges it faces as we approach the next century.

REFERENCES

Altrichter, H. & Gstettner, P. (forthcoming) 'Action research: A closed chapter in the history of German social science?', in R. McTaggart (ed.) *Participatory Action Research: Contexts and Consequences*, Deakin University, Geelong

Bell, R. (1987) *Program for Analysis of Repertory Grid Data*, Department of Psychology, Melbourne University

Daniel, W. (1990) *Applied Nonparametric Statistics*, 2nd edn, PWS-Kent, Boston

Jones, A. & May, J. (1992) *Working in Human Service Organizations*, Longman Cheshire, Melbourne

Kellehear, A. (1993) *The Unobtrusive Researcher*, Allen & Unwin, Sydney

Kelly, G. (1955) *The Psychology of Personal Construct*, Norton, New York

Schon, D. (1983) *The Reflective Practitioner*, Basic Books, New York
Stewart, A. & Barry, J. (1991) 'Origins of George Kelly's constructivism in the work of Korzybski and Moreno', *International Journal of Personal Construct Psychology*, vol. 4, pp. 121–136
Williams, A. (1989) *The Passionate Technique*, Routledge, London
Zuber-Skerritt, O. (1992) *Professional Development in Higher Education*, Kogan Page, London

9 Participation of 'the researched': Tensions between different paradigms

Linette Hawkins

In agreeing to reflect upon the research practice, theory and methods arising out of my recent research experience, I felt overwhelmed by what I perceived as a demanding intellectual challenge. Wrong! While the intellectual challenge remains, the realisation that I risk exposing many facets of my inextricably entwined personal, professional and political self leads to feelings of awe and vulnerability.

This chapter explores the insights, dilemmas, contradictions and pitfalls I faced when engaging in a qualititive longitudinal study while remaining philosophically committed to participatory action research. The longitudinal study necessitated an intermittent relationship with individual respondents to elicit a range and depth of information at different stages of their development, with little recognition or reward provided during the five-year process. In contrast, participatory action research is usually engaged in as a group activity owned by the participants, the researcher operating as joint participant–facilitator.

A critical issue for me lies in the realisation that the outcomes of both the longitudinal study on social work education and previous participatory action research I had undertaken into the training needs of the social and community services industry would have been quite different if the research models had been reversed.

This leads me to ask whether research as I practice it has become so intertwined with my values and philosophy that, operating to some extent intuitively, I am unable to stand back and critically review it. And then I realise that the problem goes beyond documenting past experience. For me it is an ongoing issue, my values interfacing with the various methods which I am adopting to also foresee the future demand for social work and community development education.

As Schon (1983, p.4) points out, we frame problematic situations in different ways, according to our disciplinary backgrounds, organisational roles, histories, interests, and political/economic perspectives. These differences are not only among us but my experience indicates that they also occur within each of us. Whenever I am challenged about the findings (by people with different values or vested interests!), or information of which I was previously unaware comes to my attention, I adapt, modify, condition or, on some occasions, change my latest interpretation of data. In this way the participatory action research approach has fitted comfortably with my social work practice, enabling me to integrate research into my everyday activities. McTaggart (1989, p.5) refers to this process as a spiral of stages through which we progress, planning, acting, observing, reflecting, re-planning for further implementation, and so on in seeking improvement or change individually or collectively.

Although this chapter focuses upon my involvement with a different kind of methodology used for a qualitative longitudinal study, the dilemmas raised cannot be divorced from my interpretations of the qualitative data, which are inextricably bound with my ideology and values. It is important therefore to contextualise these within my previous social work/research experience and identity. This may also demonstrate why my interests and values are intertwined with the research findings as well as processes.

The differences and dilemmas arising from theory underlying the qualitative longitudinal approach are explored in terms of methodology, process and analysis. This leads onto my interpretation of the long-term advantages of this approach (i.e. the qualitative approach) which fall into two main areas: those ancillary to the study (associated to some extent with the opportunity to become more interactive at the final stage) and outcomes pending action research strategies to maximise the applicability and value of findings beyond this study. The following reflections upon certain stages of my education and experience contextualise the tension arising between these two different methodologies.

RESEARCH WITH A SMALL 'R'

As a product of social work education in the late 1960s, I initially acquired a reactive approach to my work which, viewed retrospectively, attempted to address opposite ends of the continuum, with a significant gap in the middle. That is, common issues arising from individual service delivery work at one end of the continuum tended to be taken up by workers within their organisations or inter-organisationally at the other end of the continuum. Peak bodies were used to influence policy at the macro level. Consumer participation and community action (at the 'grass-roots' level) of any significance were yet to emerge.

It was towards the end of the social work course, while I was studying 'Social Organisation B' (sociology for social work students at Melbourne University), that I was introduced to theories which challenged many of those I had previously learnt and threw new light on the frustrations I had experienced practising as a novice. The sociopolitical nature of social organisation led me to adopt a crudely conceived structural approach to social work.

This approach fitted comfortably with the introduction of the Australian Assistance Plan by the federal Labor government in 1973. Working with the Department of Social Security in a rural region provided the opportunity—at least for a few years—to operate innovatively, at times proactively, engaging in strategies unforeseen in the traditional casework, group work, community organisation curriculum. Programs associated with this period enabled me to throw away the professional/consumer dichotomy, the community becoming as much a client as the individual, the social worker comfortably fitting the role of community facilitator. A workshop led by Yoland Wadsworth, author of *Do It Yourself Social Research* and founder of the Action Research Issues Centre in Melbourne, demystified research, introducing me to the participatory action research approach. This provided a model whereby individual problems might be recontextualised as community concerns, my role as facilitator enabling more effective involvement with consumers and community groups than previously. Integrating participatory action research into my role resulted in personalising my research while politicising my social work. This had a spiralling effect which reflected back to challenge social work's education and identity through the following study.

In conjunction with Yoland Wadsworth and other colleagues, I used a participatory action approach (modified) to ascertain the social and community services training needs in Victoria for the Department of Technical and Further Education (TAFE) in the 1980s. A key finding of this study was the widespread need for flexible access to education for social change and development. Employment trends associated with the Australian Social Welfare Union's move for a community development award, and the number of workers practising community development who sought a better understanding of theories related to their work, drew attention to the need for courses alternative to those based on the welfare model.

Provision of an associate diploma in community development at TAFE level, for articulation into the third year of a degree in community development, was negotiated between TAFE, two universities and the Australian Social Welfare Union, with strong support from several neighbourhood learning centres. An interesting issue debated during curriculum development for the course was the place of research as a subject. Those committed to the participatory action research approach argued for research as an integral component of the course; others believed that the acquisition of research theory and skills should occur at university, particularly at postgraduate level.

As might be expected, the attention given to community development education was viewed by some social workers as a threat or a challenge, the demand for community development workers and education reflecting to some extent negatively on the place of social work in our community. I had undertaken this work with TAFE with no strong views about the need for or importance of any particular courses in the social and community services area. However, this was to change.

Outcomes of my work with TAFE using the participatory action research approach to identify social and community service training needs increased my concern about the future of social work and changed the direction of my work. The opportunity to acquire an overview of the social and community services industry in Victoria resulted in a social work image which appeared to be shrinking, ,in inverse relation to the expansion of the community services industry. Study processes and outcomes led to a commitment to community development ideology and a recognition of the significance of the structuralist approach in challenging traditional social work education. Contrary to the community concept articulated (and to some extent applied!) during the 1970s, a large proportion of social workers either were clustered in service delivery at the micro level or had risen to managerial positions within the establishment by the mid-1980s. Graduates seeking broader roles acquired alternative titles. Consequently, although I operate as a social worker/community development worker, the positions I have held since have been designated otherwise (for example, as indicated in my work as a research assistant with Jan Fook and Martin Ryan).

THE STUDY

Several years ago I was invited by Jan Fook and Martin Ryan to carry out a component of a study aimed at charting the skill and knowledge development of social workers. The study comprised two parts—a longitudinal study of a cohort of social work students, and a study of experienced workers. I was initially involved in interviewing 30 experienced social workers, an exploratory study of their practice aimed at contributing to the development of a theory of social work expertise. The interviewing role was primarily as 'listener', obtaining background educational and occupational information, noting the responses to two vignettes, and recording their reflection upon a critical incident. Although I was initially engaged as an interviewer, my role developed into that of a co-researcher convinced of the potential value of the study and committed to pursuing the intended outcomes.

Using a qualitative approach, the longitudinal study focuses on tracing the progress of 30 social work students over a five-year period, from the start of a second degree two-year social work course at an Australian university to the end of three years practice upon graduation. The interviews, undertaken at nine stages, generally focused upon one vignette (written by the researchers) and one critical incident (experienced and selected by the respondent). Martin Ryan's chapter in this book (Chapter 10) provides more detailed documentation of the study. The aim of the study was to see whether the Dreyfus (1986) model of skills acquisition and development was applicable to skill and knowledge acquisition in social work, as well as documenting the changing features of development as a social worker over a five-year period (Fook, Ryan & Hawkins, 1994).

As the study progressed, more active participation of respondents was promoted in a variety of ways, leading to progress towards a participatory action approach following formal conclusion of the five-year project.

CONFLICTS, CONTRADICTIONS AND DILEMMAS

An ongoing dilemma arising in my interviewing role was that of the passive versus the participatory researcher. Commitment to the project's longer term goals necessitated the silence of a traditional researcher rather than response as a peer, colleague or facilitator. Aware of the importance of minimising my influence on the responses, I rigorously applied Biestek's (1961) casework principles, such as acceptance, individualisation, controlled emotional involvement, non-judgmentalism and self-determination. One might argue that this silent acceptance of all that the respondents confided risked reinforcing the views they expressed and their underlying values. Consequently I experienced tension associated with minimal participation and the power difference between respondents and researchers. Occasionally I projected this tension onto others, stimulating discussion on topics about which we shared common interests after formal questioning concluded. On some occasions I felt almost two-faced, reassuring respondents during the interview that there were no correct answers, merely different responses, and conveying symbolic supportive messages to maintain the relationship. The following section documents some of the complex issues underlying the conflicts, contradictions and dilemmas that arose during the longitudinal study.

Who are the social workers?

When we sought 'social workers with expertise' to interview we needed to define our population. Because field education staff in the social work schools are in touch with a network of practitioners, we sought a list of ten practitioners from each school esteemed by staff for their competence. Although a number of those interviewed held jobs with other designated titles, most had accessed these positions through their social work qualifications, were working with other social workers, and indicated ongoing commitment to social work through their contribution to field education.

Interviewing social workers recommended by the schools meant that we risked restricting ourselves to those likely to be in more conventional social work positions, since these were the workers who might typically take students on placement. The question arises whether we should have ensured that we researched the expertise of social workers engaged in diverse positions, the nature of whose work may have precluded their involvement in more conventional field education placements.

This question is particularly pertinent at a time when designated social work positions are diminishing in number. Trends within the social and community services industry in Victoria during the past decade reflect a range of factors contributing to the decline in demand for social workers. These factors include recognition of the industry by TAFE (in the mid-1980s), resulting in an increase in paraprofessional community services courses and the formation of an industry training board; deregulation of previously defined social work positions in the public sector to accommodate a wider range of graduates; an increase in 'community-based' positions (often part-time, casual or temporary) associated with the de-institutionalisation of services; limited access to social work education for experienced but unqualified workers in rural areas and/or requiring more flexible study programs. Social work education in Victoria is being challenged from both ends of the spectrum. An increase in welfare courses (particularly at degree level) raises competition within the social welfare establishment, while community development graduates are sought after by an increasing number of community-based organisations.

Passive versus participatory process

Only one of the recommended field educators declined the invitation to participate in the exploratory study of experienced social workers. The willingness of others to contribute to the study almost unquestioningly was encouraging, a minority seeking feedback about its progress.

This willingness to give with no immediate visible reward also stood out during interviews with respondents inthe remaining stages of the study. Interviewing participants every six months and then once a year heightened my sensitivity to their attitudes, values and feelings, resulting in an unusual kind of rapport.

Tensions varied throughout the three-year period of my involvement. My desire to respond to issues confronting respondents at each stage balanced as the study progressed and I became aware of the significance of 'holding back', observing over time the personal/professional changes resulting mainly from a combination of the education they had received and the environment in which they were working. I have referred to the differences observed in respondents at stages after graduation as personal/professional changes rather than personal/professional development as the latter implies general progress of respondents towards the next level of competence. This fails to take account of the situation of some respondents, who questioned whether their positions and environment enabled them to practise social work, or even operate professionally, since the tightly programmed role of workers in some bureaucracies counteracts the notions of autonomy and power associated with expertise and traditional professionalism. These respondents are part of an increasing number of graduate social workers who find themelves at the opposite end of the continuum to those who were interviewed for their experience and expertise.

The frustration I felt related more to my own values than to those of the respondents. I was constantly surprised by their unquestioning acceptance of their ongoing role as subjects in a longitudinal study. This also contrasted with the interest aroused in third-year community development students at another university when, as a separate 'pilot' study, their written responses to one of the vignettes were obtained. The community development students' demand for feedback and the opportunity to pursue implications of the findings contrasted significantly with the ongoing acceptance of input without follow-up shown by the longitudinal study participants. Even more frustrating for me was the way in which a number of graduates seemed to accept either unquestioningly or with resignation their restricted, and in some instances clearly defined, social-control roles.

The fine line I was treading, intermittently taking information but returning little, was overstepped when, about two-thirds of the way through, expressions of interest in feedback were received from a small number of respondents. I supported their case and agreed to take the matter up with my colleagues instead of entering into discussion about parameters implied in a study of this nature. This placed us in a difficult situation, deciding upon the type of information to communicate without significantly influencing future stages of the study. The summary we eventually mailed out aroused the anger of those actively seeking feedback, who considered the contents superficial and unrelated to their personal contribution.

In a sense our research methodology may have contributed to a kind of self-fulfilling prophecy. While collecting data on the skill and knowledge development of a cohort of social work students to use in developing a theory of social work expertise, we intermittently interacted with them on a one-to-one basis. Moreover, as mentioned above, we retained tight control of the information gathered, at least until the final stage. This raises a question regarding the extent to which we as researchers have unintentionally reinforced a major finding of the study, that an individualising approach seems to dominate this group's conceptualisation and contextualisation of social work (Fook *et al.*, 1994, p.11)

The above incident provided a clear example of how, during a study applying an interpretive approach, one must be cautious about changing strategy midway. Fortunately, our relationship with respondents was able to ride this hiccup, the more vocal participants now playing an active role in outcomes arising from the study, referred to below.

An interesting contrast to the above incident arose when, at the end-of-study dinner attended by most participants, we distributed copies of the recently published article 'Becoming a social worker' (Fook *et al.*, 1994). The lack of feedback from participants to date raises further interesting questions related to and extending beyond the individualised approach.

Perceiving myself as a passive interviewer using an interpretive approach to research, I was overlooking the more subtle side benefits gained by respondents. This became more obvious at the final interview, when respondents in stressful situations shared their thoughts and feelings when describing their critical incident, saying they appreciated the opportunity to ventilate them. This leads to the realisation that reflection upon one's work with a non-judgmental listener is highly valued, especially by workers with little likelihood of being listened to or opportunity to reflect on anything other than the tasks for which they are responsible, or who are ambivalent about those in authority. During Stage 9 (the interview concluding the five-year study), the off-site listener role of the inter-viewer/researcher was particularly valued by a few respondents, especially those who had recently undergone crisis, were in conflict with superiors or, in a few instances, were at a turning point in their career.

Reliability and validity

The difficulties arising from concentrated listening and comprehens-ive recording during interviews, although never resolved, were partly addressed by developing my own version of shorthand. An issue not yet tackled, but which becomes relevant to our current analysis of the language and terminology used by social workers, relates to the tendency of other interviewers in the early stages to record interviews in summarised note form, often paraphrasing subjects' responses rather than recording them verbatim. For me the actual words used by the respondent are critical. When possible, all my interviews have been taken down verbatim in shorthand to maximise accuracy.

This also raises a question about the validity of the responses. The information provided by respondents is of a secondary nature, informing us how they think they would respond to certain case situations and what they perceive to have been their thoughts, feelings, fears and behaviour in critical instances. Our written record constitutes a further sifting of data. Analysis could thus be viewed as the fourth stage of interpretation of an abbreviated record (third stage) of the respondent's articulation (second stage) of their action or likely role. Consequently, the distance between respondents' actions and researchers' analysis must be acknowledged.

An alternative method for studying the application of knowledge and skills was that used with social work graduates of the Carleton University in Canada to define the characteristics of their structural approach by gathering examples and illustrations from their practice (Moreau et al., 1993). As well as interviewing the individual worker, researchers acquired tapes of client–worker interviews, providing them with more direct access to the data.

While this method provides a more accurate image of worker interaction with the consumer, the advantage of the longitudinal nature of our study lies in the issue of consistency or otherwise throughout the nine stages. Moreover, the critical incidents provided an opportunity for respondents to reflect upon the many types of social work practices and processes in which they were engaged, extending beyond interaction with a consumer.

Although detailed note-taking of responses to the standard

questions was customary at each interview, I felt a strong ambivalence towards recording observations which appeared ancillary to the
primary focus (that is, comments on case vignettes and critical
incidents). On occasions when I surreptitiously jotted down my
observations, I experienced pangs of guilt, as though I had trans-
gressed the unspoken boundaries. In some instances this behaviour
confirmed the impression conveyed in the main content of the
interview; on other occasions, it contradicted it. Examples include
the respondent who was constantly yawning, another who whispered
negative comments about the section head who interrupted the
interview, and the person developing a career alternative to their
full-time position with the public service.

Data analysis

I was initially overwhelmed by the privilege of participating in a
significant academic study, and, loaded from an early stage with
reams of data, I pursued or rather tried to follow my colleagues in
undertaking a pure content analysis, using clear categories and
counting instances of data falling into each category. This more
quantitative approach led me into the trap of finding a framework
for categorising 'hard data'. I shudder to think of the time spent
(wasted?) setting up schedules for dissecting the responses to each
question and sorting them into the 35 main points grouped under
material/physical, psychological, social and structural aspects—all
borrowed from clinical studies and with limited relevance to the roles
of our respondents. Or, in another instance, analysing the reasons
given for studying social work in terms of personal, professional,
educational and experiential categories.

Encumbered with huge amounts of data, I sifted it for semi-quan-
titative outcomes, selecting a particular question, collating all
responses, then drawing out common or contrasting factors across
vignettes, among respondents, creating grids of statistics for categories of critical incidents. The 'aha!' sensations were few and far
between, but in the long run the 'search for quantitative material'
provided evidence for broader issues which stood out later when I
adopted a qualitative approach.

A less successful application of a more quantitative approach was
an attempt to identify the theories reflected by 'expert' social workers
when recalling a critical incident. Fifteen different theories were noted
among half the responses, the theoretical approach of the other half
was unclear!

A more quantitative approach was perhaps most useful in analysing the degree of intervention (or action plan) articulated in responses
to case vignettes. Using the stages through which a worker proceeds

from assessment to termination as a scale for crudely defining the nature and degree of intervention articulated by subjects in both studies allowed us to compare the two groups as well as trace the progress along the scale of respondents at different points in the longitudinal study.

As indicated in Chapter 10, we progressed from a content analysis approach to using inductive and deductive methods for analysis, a model which provided greater flexibility, allowing us to explore our material in both interpretive and quantitative ways.

In participatory action research and as a practitioner, I contextualise myself by 'starting where the particular person or community is at', drawing from their information and my observations. Interpretation of the findings in this approach is part of an ongoing collective process, integrated into and arising out of the data collection. In contrast, the analysis of our empirical study has been dependent on the interpretive approaches of our small team. Whereas Martin and Jan tended to use social work theory and educational frameworks to help them conceptualise and articulate the data, my experience relates to contextualising social work within a sociopolitical framework.

Consequently I have felt that my attempt at data analysis has been organised chaos, the organisation obtained in meetings with my two colleagues, the chaos from interchanging the deductive and inductive approaches and alternating between educational, industrial and ideological frames of reference. In other words, I sought data to support, or refute, the Dreyfus model of knowledge and skills acquisition (the five stages of development from novice to expert) and diverted to an inductive approach when I discovered evidence to support my own frame of reference!

An ongoing tension arising from the educator, or academic, versus practitioner frame of reference relates to the implications of the longitudinal study findings for the issue of social work's image versus education for social work. Aiming at exploring implications for social work education, I tended to focus on the significance of the findings for the future of social work as an occupation.

Theory in use

As indicated in the above dilemmas, our shared espoused theory of interpretive qualitative interviewing and analysis at the early stages led to feelings of tension with my previous participatory action research experience. Reflecting on this, it appears that the minor but negative outcome (referred to earlier) of our token feedback two-thirds of the way through, and at my instigation, confronted me with problems arising from this ambivalence.

As the longitudinal study progressed, opportunites for more active participation of respondents were promoted in a variety of ways, leading to a participatory action research phase following the formal conclusion of the project. Involvement in the longitudinal study has given me insight into and allowed me to reflect upon the complexities of issues which I am committed to and seek to change while also providing evidence and accessing resources to address this.

A theoretical challenge we now face is how to supplement our research with a comparative study so we may begin to distinguish the local from the more universal in our findings. It is likely that associated research will be constrained by time. Future approaches should perhaps take more account of ways to reward participants for their commitment and contribution.

Perhaps the greatest challenge will be to design a more mixed model of research, promoting participation and more equal interaction without interfering with or influencing the development of the key characteristics under study.

UNINTENDED OUTCOMES

Although the study formally closed only recently, it has had many unforeseen outcomes. Several participants expressed regret that the study was drawing to an end. During the final stage of interviewing, respondents were invited to indicate whether they were interested in a further stage in which they would participate in writing a book reflecting upon their entire learning experience.

The response to the ancillary pilot study with community development students referred to earlier has led us to realise the importance of terminology relating to social justice and its application. We are currently exploring this and its implications for future teaching.

Impressions gained from this study reinforced my concerns about the place and direction of social work education. In conjunction with several colleagues keen to bring greater accountability to schools of social work, I have been involved in forming a special-interest group under the auspices of the professional association. The group has recently attracted a few of the longitudinal study respondents, women who wanted to have greater influence upon their social work course.

Other discourse has led to at least two respondents applying to undertake postgraduate studies.

Two of us (researchers) have recently been involved in the writing and establishment of a new social work course. Our experiences in undertaking this study have significantly influenced aspects of the curriculum content and design.

Papers presented on the project to date have stimulated the interest of other social work educators and have the potential to influence the national professional association's forthcoming review of the ways in which social work courses are accredited.

The critical challenge facing us now is how we may extend our study and analyse findings which are applicable to a wider population. This requires the attention of key players within both social work education and higher education generally.

CONCLUSION

A number of the dilemmas referred to in this chapter reflect upon social work and social work education in general. What does our individualist approach to obtaining information throughout the study say about our approach to working with people? On the other hand, one might argue the inappropriateness of seeking contact in any other form, the respondents never presenting as an identifiable group— beyond the fact that they were all enrolled in the same social work course. Perhaps this factor justifies generalisation beyond the respondents to the broader social work student population, placing primary attention upon the effects of their education and changes required by consumers and the community.

My commitment to broader objectives, seeking evidence to support my concerns, often resulted in diverting our collaborative attention from the principal aim of the study—to delineate skill and knowledge development—to my personal agenda: to change social work education and practice.

Our contrasting starting points highlighted different perspectives throughout the study which became more convergent in the later stages. The researchers set out with a relatively open mind regarding likely outcomes. In contrast, I came in as an interviewer with a desire to see changes in social work's identity reinforced by concerns about the increasingly conservative profile of social work which were backed by outcomes of the participatory action approach to TAFE planning. Consequently I had certain values and concerns about social work education and was seeking evidence to support or challenge them.

My seeming obsession with the non-participatory approach to respondents has been more than compensated for by the open communication and acceptance of each other's values in our three-person collaborative team. Working with two committed, experienced 'expert' academics has provided not only inestimable knowledge but also role models, adding to the small number of mentors I have 'collected' and challenging my ambivalence about the future of social work. The process of reflecting upon conflicts, dilemmas and contradictions arising out of this study has reaffirmed my commitment to research which has the potential to change social work education.

REFERENCES

Biestek, F. (1961) *The Casework Relationship*, Allen & Unwin, London

Dreyfus, H. & Dreyfus, S. (1986) *Mind Over Machine: The Power of Human Intuition and Expertise in the Era of the Computer*, Basil Blackwell, Oxford

Fook, J., Ryan, M. & Hawkins, L, (1994) 'Becoming a social worker: Some educational implications from preliminary findings of a longitudinal study', *Social Work Education*, vol.13, no.2, July, pp. 5–26

McTaggart, R. (1989) 'Principles for participatory action research', a paper presented to the Third World Encounter on Participatory Research, Manuagua, Nicaragua

Moreau, M., Frosst, S., Frayne, G., *et al.*, (1993) *Empowerment 11, Snapshots of the Structural Approach in Action*, Carleton University, Canada

Schon, D. (1983) *The Reflective Practitioner*, Basic Books, New York

Wadsworth, Y. (1984), *Do It Yourself Social Research*, Victorian Council of Social Service, Melbourne Family Care Organisation, Collingwood, Victoria

10 Doing longitudinal research: A personal reflection

Martin Ryan

Most people are familiar with the *Seven Up* documentary series directed by Michael Apted in which a group of British children from different social classes is interviewed about its expectations, values and attitudes at seven-year intervals over 28 years. The series is an example of a type of longitudinal-panel study whose design is similar to that of the research study that is the focus of this chapter.

The *Seven Up* study illustrates the central principles of longitudinal research in which data is collected at more than one point in time and is designed to enable recording of variations in the same data over time. In a panel design, data is collected from the same people.

A considerable amount of research in the social sciences in general is cross-sectional, whereby a phenomenon is examined at one point in time. Longitudinal studies are less common. They are relatively rare in social work and even rarer in social work practice research. (There are some exceptions to this, such as the five-year study of children in foster care by Fanshel and Shinn (1978) and the longitudinal research in the area of social worker burn-out (Poulin & Walter, 1993).

I think there are a number of reasons for the dearth of such studies in social work: they tend to be expensive; excessively time-consuming; can pose extensive logistical difficulties and require carefully developed methods of observation and analysis (Lawton & Herzog, 1989).

The primary virtue of longitudinal research is that it enables change and the change process over time to be documented, observed

111

and analysed. It is perhaps surprising that such studies are not used more often in social work research, as social work is usually vitally concerned with change in individuals, groups, families and communities. Longitudinal research can be particularly helpful in addressing issues of causality. Cross-sectional studies assume phenomena are stable, but as social workers well know, they can change dramatically.

This chapter outlines my experience of being involved in a five-year qualitative longitudinal study with two co-researchers (Jan Fook and Linette Hawkins). This study followed a panel of beginning social work students through their two years of study and the first three years of practice with the aim of charting their skill and knowledge development (Fook, Ryan & Hawkins, 1994; Ryan, Fook & Hawkins, 1995). In the course of this chapter, a number of issues will be discussed which influenced the development of my own 'theory of action' of doing longitudinal research within a collaborative team, based on the 'reflection-in-action' model of Aygyris and Schon (1974) and Schon (1983). I will outline the study, then examine my transition to being a qualitative researcher from being a primarily quantitative one. I will then trace the 'espoused theory' of undertaking the longitudinal research and the 'theory in use' identified from experience of dealing with the opportunities and challenges of such research. Next, I will present my 'theory of action' of collaborative team research. The lessons we learnt about applying for a research grant for the project are covered in the concluding section of the chapter.

BECOMING A SOCIAL WORKER—THE LONGITUDINAL STUDY

This study arose directly out of my personal interest in how a person becomes a social worker. From the time I was a student on field education placements, I had observed very skilled and competent social workers in practice and wondered how they had managed to become so. What was the process involved? I had stored this away as something I would like to research someday.

A framework for undertaking such a study was developed by an academic in the discipline of nursing, Dr Patricia Benner. In her book *From Novice to Expert: Excellence and Power in Clinical Nursing Practice* (1984), she explored the development and complexity of expert-level nursing practice. She described the progression from the halting, rule-bound performance of the novice nurse to the holistic, seemingly intuitive performance of the expert nurse. Her thinking derived from a model of skill acquisition and development posited by Dreyfus and Dreyfus (1986) in which a student passes through five levels of proficiency: 1) novice; 2) advanced beginner; 3) competent; 4) proficient and 5) expert.

Benner tested the applicability of this model to nursing by trying to assess the differences in clinical performance and situation appraisal of beginning and expert nurses by interviewing pairs of nurses (one a beginning nurse and the other recognised for her expertise). Each member of the pair was interviewed separately about patient care situations they had in common and which stood out for them (so-called critical incidents). Both were asked for the clinical knowledge they had found particularly difficult to teach or learn. If there were differences between the two levels of nurses' accounts, how could these be accounted for and understood?

This research seemed to offer exciting applications to social work, so I approached Jan Fook, a fellow lecturer at the institution where we both taught at the time, about working and collaborating on a piece of research using Benner's framework and methodology. I knew she was particularly interested in social work practice, especially from a radical casework focus (Fook, 1993). She was also very enthusiastic about it and we started to develop the research plan from there.

Very early in our thinking, we realised that if we intended to replicate Benner's method with paired social workers (students and more experienced workers) it would be very difficult to get views from both of the same critical incident and for them not to have discussed that incident (as required by Benner). It was then that we thought about doing a longitudinal study of social work students from the beginning of their social work education through to practice and beyond. We decided to use critical incidents as a major indication of movement from level to level of the Dreyfus stages. In using a longitudinal study, we also would be extending the limited amount of longitudinal research done in the area of the development of social work students and new graduates (O'Connor, Dagleish & Khan, 1984; Harre Hindmarsh, 1992; Secker, 1993).

The aim of the study was to see whether the Dreyfus model was applicable to skill and knowledge acquisition in social work, as well as to document the changing features of social workers' development over a five-year period. We decided to follow a panel of 39 social work students from the beginning of their social work course at the university where we were lecturing through the two years of the course and the first three years of practice. The study started at the beginning of 1990 and concluded at the end of 1994 with 30 participants. We aimed to interview participants at half-yearly intervals. They were asked on each occasion to describe and discuss critical incidents chosen by them from their course experience and subsequent practice and to respond to social work practice vignettes developed by us, as well as to answer additional questions at various stages.

The interviews in the first year of the study were conducted by Jan and myself. In the following year, research assistants were employed to conduct some of the interviews. Linette Hawkins was one of these and she was eventually to become a collaborator in the research study. The research was done on an unfunded basis for the first year; for the second year it was funded by the School of Behavioural Sciences at La Trobe University (where Jan had taken up employment) and then for the final three years was funded by the Australian Research Council (ARC) from the small grants funding scheme.

At the time of writing, the study has just been completed. The five years have come and gone surprisingly quickly. We have presented our preliminary findings at national and international conferences and also published them. (For readers who are interested, these can be found in Fook *et al.*, 1994 and Ryan *et al.*, 1995.) The next stage for the study is to complete the analysis of all the data, involve the participants more directly in discussion of the findings and write a book based on the whole study in 1996.

THE TRANSITION FROM QUANTITATIVE TO QUALITATIVE RESEARCH

We decided at the outset to pursue the research using a qualitative approach. Given the study's origins in the work of Benner, a quantitative approach seemed to be neither indicated nor appropriate. Quantitative instruments were also not available to measure what we wanted in terms of social work students' skill and knowledge development to enable continuous/interval data to be generated. We were also keen to chart the development of the participants, and since little previous research had been conducted in this area this seemed to lend itself more readily to a qualitative approach.

Much of the literature on longitudinal research has a quantitative focus. For example, Menard (1991), even when writing about methods of analysis for qualitative/categorical data, concentrates on quantitative-based methods such as log-linear analysis and multistate life table models. Event history analysis, which corresponds to critical incident analysis, only receives a passing mention. So there was little guidance to be received from longitudinal research books.

My previous research education in psychology, sociology and in social work research methods had been primarily quantitative. I had used quantitative methods extensively in my postgraduate research work. A new and different way of thinking was required for qualitative research. Quantitative methods provide a clear-cut, structured approach to research. Hypotheses are generated after the completion of a literature review and the absorption and utilisation of appropriate theory. They are then subjected to empirical testing. Analysis is next undertaken using predetermined statistical tests, often with the aid of a computer.

Instead, we had a highly unstructured process. We had no hypotheses. We had a method for collecting data (interviews), and analysis was to be done by looking at what we had and analysing its content. This was not the way I had been taught at all! Here there simply would be no clear-cut results to say we had proven what we set out to establish.

Data collection via interviews was something that I was familiar with, but what did we do once we collected all the data? How did we make sense of it? These became crucial questions. As Miles (1979) has written:

> The most serious and central difficulty in the use of qualitative data is that methods of analysis are not well formulated . . . the analyst faced with a bank of qualitative data has very few guidelines for protection against self-delusion, let alone the presentation of unreliable or invalid conclusions to scientific or policy-making bodies. (p. 590)

We were eventually to impose some order on the analysis when we went back and looked at the objectives of the research. These were: 1) to look for characteristics of the Dreyfus model and 2) to trace the characteristics of the process. We had started by doing purely content analysis, but were less than happy with the results as it still produced a mass of information. This was to become the inductive or grounded-theory part of the analysis, corresponding to the second objective. We realised that we also had to examine the congruence of the collected data with the stages and characteristics of the Benner and Dreyfus model. So we decided to also use a deductive technique to analyse the data. The sorts of questions this technique sought to answer were: How was our own data different from the model? How was it similar? At what stages of the model were our participants?

Our 'mixed model' of data analysis using both inductive and deductive methods has, in fact, worked very well and in effect became our 'theory in use' for analysis. It gave a structure to the data analysis and yet allowed the data to speak for itself. Yet, as far as I am aware, no research textbook suggests this as a way of proceeding with data analysis.

We were concerned about the problem of inter-rater reliability in terms of the data analysis. Generally, this problem is associated with observation in data collection where there may be error due to observer bias. But for us, it became more of an issue in analysis, that is, a question of whether we were all interpreting and drawing similar conclusions from the recorded data. The way we attempted to address this was by having all three of the researchers read and analyse the transcripts independently and then meet to discuss their interpretations. Only after discussion and when there was consensus would a particular interpretation or conclusion be adopted as our collective view.

Another difficulty I had to overcome lay in accepting that qualitative research involved uncertainty, or at least never reaching complete answers with absolute certainty. For a qualitative researcher, there was still a constant search for meaning and explanation in a mass of data.

TOWARDS A THEORY OF ACTION OF LONGITUDINAL RESEARCH

Longitudinal research tends to get only passing and brief discussion in research textbooks. There is a small amount of specialist literature on the subject (Markus, 1979; Goldstein, 1979; Plewis, 1985; Menard, 1991), and many of these works focus on the complexities of the analysis of quantitative longitudinal data. But for social workers wanting to do practice research using a longitudinal design and a qualitative approach, there is little practical advice or 'espoused theory' available.

The 'espoused theory' of longitudinal research, in its simplest form, is outlined by Bouma (1993) when he describes the process of doing a longitudinal study as: 1) select variables relevant to the concepts under study; 2) devise a way of measuring these variables; 3) develop a data recording device and 4) measure the same variables in the same way in one group (or one person) at two or more times (p. 96).

Unfortunately, the reality was not quite as simple as this. As mentioned previously, longitudinal research has a number of distinct advantages and disadvantages. The two combine to produce the unique opportunities and challenges of this type of research. Any 'theory in use' or 'theory in action' needs to take account of the particular challenges posed by longitudinal research. I will outline my version of these two theories based on the experience of undertaking this study.

My 'theory in use' would emphasise that one of the most significant issues for a piece of longitudinal research is panel attrition, or the loss of respondents as time goes on. We were fortunate in being able to retain 30 of the original 39 participants selected for the study at its beginning in 1990. Thirty-nine had been selected as a sufficient number to ensure a significant range of students and to allow for an attrition rate of up to 25 per cent over the course of the study. Those who withdrew from the study did so for a number of reasons: withdrawal or deferment from the course; an intention to work interstate or overseas; and, after graduating, being unable or choosing not to work as a social worker.

We were able to enthuse the participants initially about being in the study. We spoke to them as a group at the conclusion of their first class in one of their subjects, which one of us taught, and asked for their participation in the study. We stressed the uniqueness of the study in that it was a five-year longitudinal study of beginning social work students. This struck a chord, and fortunately, they all agreed to participate.

The retention rate was even more surprising given that we gave the participants very little feedback during the study. The feedback we did give consisted of some very general findings and observations and details of any papers that were being presented or published from the study. We did this deliberately in order to minimise our influence on their responses, thereby reducing undue biasing of any findings. This posed great difficulties for us as researchers as we were keen to share our findings with the participants, and it clearly smacked of research at its worst—passive subjects who are manipulated in the interests of 'science' by supposedly 'objective' scientific researchers without being informed about the researchers' purposes.

The retention rate was also surprising in view of the fact that the interviews in the first two years were conducted by two of the participants' lecturers, who were also involved in assessing them as part of their duties. This was, in fact, an issue raised by the university's ethics committee when we sought permission to undertake the study. We dealt with it in a number of ways:

1 Stressing that Jan and I were not involved in any teaching in field education subjects nor were we undertaking any student placement liaison, where impressions we had formed as a result of the study might have been brought to bear, either consciously or not.
2 Taking care that we did not discuss the results of our data collection with any other member of the teaching staff of the department.
3 Reassuring the students about these two points and that data from the study would not affect any assessment in the course.

This problem was allayed to a large extent when they had completed their degrees and were freed from the university's scrutiny. It was also lessened by having research assistants doing the interviewing who were not associated with either the course or the university.

Other factors also operated, in my view, to aid retention of participants. The study gave them the opportunity to debrief from their placement and work experience with someone who was a social worker and yet not directly involved in any evaluation of them. In addition, all interviewers were under instructions not to respond in any way which could be interpreted as judgmental. There was also the element of valuing the continuing contact with the university where they had obtained their social work qualification. Also, involvement in the study entailed primarily a once- or twice-yearly interview, which at worst could be considered a minor inconvenience.

We were generally easily able to maintain contact with participants, as the interviews were relatively frequent with at least yearly contact. We obtained their home addresses and addresses of parents if need be. We also used annual mailings in the form of Christmas cards to maintain contact with participants. These measures all proved effective, combined with the fact that many of the participants knew each other and were able to supply us with, for example, changes of work addresses of other participants.

While the data collection was certainly constant, the greater difficulty was keeping up with its analysis. Our focus was very much on the interviewing, but a definite plan of action and commitment to undertaking ongoing analysis needed to be built in at the outset. This is particularly so with qualitative research, which can generate a vast amount of data. We at times fell badly behind on the analysis.

A commonly reported problem in the longitudinal research literature (Menard, 1991) is that the repeated measurement required can produce panel conditioning. Such conditioning may result in the tendency of respondents to answer questions in such a way as to produce a known response. Respondents can also become more sensitive to their own behaviour and values. It may be that this produces noticeable changes in values and behaviour.

Certainly our participants became habituated to the critical-incident format. This was a concern for us and we attempted to overcome it by altering the intervals between data-collection times (from twice a year to three times a year for two years to once a year for the final two years of the study); by small variations in each data-collection stage in the vignettes and additional questions (but not the critical incident, which retained a consistent format), so that at each stage participants could expect both consistency and some degree of unpredictability and variety.

Difficulty with respondent recall, another common problem in longitudinal research, was minimised by asking them to select a critical incident from recent practice. Often this meant that incidents within two to four weeks of the interview were selected.

In summary, my 'theory of action' of longitudinal research would stress a number of points: 1) retention of participants is crucial and great pains should be taken to really engage them in a truly collaborative way; 2) time for data analysis as well as collection should be built into the research plan; 3) a model of data analysis that fits the aims of the study is what will work for you, such as our 'mixed model'.

COLLABORATIVE TEAM RESEARCH

Collaborative team research was as new to me as was qualitative research. As my previous research had been conducted alone, this was also a major transition for me. My previous experiences with working on group research projects as an undergraduate social work student were less than happy, as they had been characterised by personality clashes and conflict, members of the group not doing their fair share of the work and difficulties getting the final product completed on time. My experiences were not a positive foundation to work on.

When Linette Hawkins became a collaborator in the study, Jan and I agreed that we very much wanted her to assume this role. Although her involvement began and continues as that of a paid research assistant, she also contributed much to both the analysis and generation of ideas arising from the study, as well as conducting the bulk of the interviewing.

The way we have divided tasks tended to vary with the job at hand. The joint sessions when we came together to discuss our interpretations of the interview data were also a time for 'brainstorming' new ideas, which might originate from one person, with confirmation then coming from the others. At times, work was done only jointly, for example, when developing a conference paper abstract. At other times, one of us took responsibility for writing a draft and then the other two offered critical comments on it.

Initially, when writing conference papers or articles, we had equal responsibility in writing them. After discussion, we would each undertake to write particular sections, for example the literature review, results or discussion sections. We would then comment on each other's section. As time went on, we modified that style slightly in order to optimise efficiency and output. Now one person takes responsibility for the whole of a piece of work and the others provide input on this. The key point in ensuring harmony is that any division of labour is worked out beforehand and all members of the team agree with it.

In retrospect, I think this combination of the three of us as a collaborative research team has worked particularly well and the teamwork is something we should feel proud of. It may also serve as a valuable lesson from which others can draw, particularly when teamwork produces horror stories of constant conflict and difficulties. It is not surprising that such efforts end badly when one thinks of their genesis. A number of work colleagues get on well together and may even be close friends outside work. They may have very similar ideas and thoughts. Some 'espoused theory' would suggest that this may seem to them an ideal basis for collaborating on some research they may be interested in. This is the first mistake. *Never* assume that goodwill and friendship will carry over into a collaborative working relationship. It is a good basis but, based on my experience, much more is required.

My 'theory of action' would incorporate the following two-stage process for successful collaborative research team relationships:

1 Developing criteria to be used in selecting collaborators and then seeing if possible collaborators can meet these criteria.
2 Once you are satisfied about this and collaborators have been selected, then a working agreement/contract needs to be drawn up and agreed to by all parties. It would include such matters as timelines, methods of dealing with disagreements; division of work load; possible avenues of publication and authorship questions.

The criteria for selection of collaborators could include some or all of the following:

1 *Publishing and writing track record.* Does the person have a track record? It may not be in the form of published work, but may be an honours or postgraduate thesis or an unpublished report. You may want to read samples of their work.
2 *Philosophical and ideological compatibility.* Where another's views are diametrically and implacably opposed to your own this is unlikely to produce a satisfactory working relationship. Similar perspectives on research and theoretical approaches would appear to work best.
3 *Technical and practical skills.* The other person may not be able to do everything that you can, but their skills should be complementary and be able to contribute to the overall research project.
4 *Similar ethical standards in relation to research.*
5 *Writing style compatibility.* Is their style compatibile with yours?

Who is to have the final veto on writing style? Such questions are closely connected with authorship issues.

6 *Availability*. Is this other person happy to be contacted in the evenings or at weekends if you want to discuss the research or to work on it? How much intrusion into their personal life is admissible?

7 *Ability to meet deadlines*. There is nothing worse than the constant procrastinator who never seems to produce the goods.

The question of authorship deserves special attention because it can potentially be a source of great conflict. This is possibly related to the politics of authorship as interpreted by university committees for promotion and/or tenure with multi-authored works before them. If there are more than two authors of a work, often only the first is cited, with the others becoming *et al*. For such committees, there is an innate difficulty determining the proportion of a particular author's contribution to the total work. The question then becomes: How do co-authors decide on the order in which their names will appear? We adopted the simple principle that the person who made the greatest contribution to the publication be named first. In our case, this has generally been a clear-cut decision. This issue is decided and agreed to at the beginning of the writing process rather than at the end, when there is more likely to be injured feelings and conflict. Again the important thing is to establish the rule in advance. Dunkin (1992) suggests a range of rules for deciding the order of authors' names, from co-authors taking it in turns to student authors being named first, to a coin being tossed.

The rewards of collaborative research are important to stress. The opportunity for discussing ideas in a collaborative and supportive environment is stimulating, exhilarating, productive and ultimately results in a better finished product than a solo effort would. Our best work has been done sitting together tossing ideas around in an almost haphazard way. It can really serve to stimulate whole new trains of thought. Other advantages are that it can increase one's publication output considerably and provides ready evidence that one can work collaboratively. The standard of the work each of us has produced has certainly been enhanced by being read and constructively criticised by two other people. In short, the rewards are there, provided one sets up the rules at the outset to ensure that the team will function properly.

OBTAINING RESEARCH FUNDING

Longitudinal research is expensive given the length of time over which the study may be conducted. This really necessitates some sort of research-grant funding, which can be very difficult to obtain. We managed to do the research unfunded for the first year, with Jan Fook and I conducting all the data collection and analysis. After that we were able to obtain funding, which enabled us to employ research assistants to assist with interviewing and analysis. Winning research funding becomes even more difficult when the research is qualitative and has what can be perceived as unclear aims and objectives as opposed to precisely developed hypotheses. Traditionally, social work has found it difficult to attract ARC funding under either the large or small grant funding schemes. For example, in 1993, only two ARC large grants and six small grants were awarded to staff working in Australian departments of social work (Australian Research Council, 1993).

Rather than go into the intricacies and details of writing a good research submission or proposal, I refer readers to Roberts's book (1993) or the article by Leukefield and Ries (1993). I will just make a few simple points that we have found to be useful.

1 Lacking a research track record in the area to be researched can be problematic, but can be compensated for by a willingness to set up and undertake research on an unfunded basis. Seeding or starter grants may be an appropriate source.
2 Demonstrate the value of your unfunded research by the completion and presentation of conference papers and articles, preferably in international refereed journals.
3 Have someone on the relevant research committee who is familiar with the research, is convinced of its merit and is prepared to advocate that it to be funded or be granted further funding.
4 Clearly spell out what the proposed study involves and how it is useful. This is actually quite difficult and requires considerable time and care.
5 Practice and persistence are important, and so is advice from peers and colleagues.
6 There is a need to always be thinking about and planning the next research grant submission.

CONCLUSION

As a result of this longitudinal study, we have been able to see the process of becoming a social worker at work. We have been able to observe and chart the characteristics and manifestations of development and growth and change, even if we have not always been able to delineate the precise causes of such change. The insights we obtained would not have been possible with a cross-sectional study.

I have outlined 'theories of action' for both longitudinal research and collaborative team research. Both tasks can be fraught with pitfalls and potential difficulties, and not all of these can be anticipated, but with due planning and forethought in the ways I have suggested many of these can be met and overcome to make longitudinal research using a collaborative team approach an exciting and productive practice research endeavour.

NOTE

This chapter has benefited from discussions with Jan Fook, Linette Hawkins, Yvonne Roddy, Janet Patford and Daphne Habibis, particularly in relation to collaborative team research.

REFERENCES

Argyris, C. & Schon, D. (1974) *Theory in Practice: Increasing Professional Effectiveness*, Jossey-Bass, San Francisco

Australian Research Council, Department of Employment, Education and Training (1994) *Report on Research Funding Programs 1993*, Australian Government Publishing Service, Canberra

Benner, P. (1984) *From Novice to Expert: Excellence and Power in Clinical Nursing Practice*, Addison-Wesley, Menlo Park, California

Bouma, G. (1993) *The Research Process*, rev. edn, Oxford University Press, Melbourne

Dreyfus, H. & Dreyfus, S. (1986) *Mind Over Machine: The Power of Human Intuition and Expertise in the Era of the Computer*, Basil Blackwell, Oxford

Dunkin, M. (1992) 'Some dynamics of authorship', *Australian Universities' Review*, vol.35, no.1, pp. 43–48

Fanshel, D. & Shinn, E. (1978) *Children in Foster Care: A Longitudinal Investigation*, Columbia University Press, New York

Fook, J. (1993) *Radical Casework*, Allen & Unwin, Sydney

Fook, J., Ryan, M. & Hawkins, L. (1994) 'Becoming a social worker: Some educational implications from preliminary findings of a longitudinal study', *Social Work Education*, vol.13, no.2, July, pp. 5–26

Goldstein, H. (1979) *The Design and Analysis of Longitudinal Studies*, Academic Press, New York

Harre Hindmarsh, J. (1992) *Social Work Oppositions*, Avebury, Aldershot

Lawton, M. & Herzog, R. (1989) (eds) *Special Research Methods for Gerontology*, Baywood, New York

Leukefeld, C. & Ries, J. (1993) 'Strategies to compete for federal grant funding for research on social work practice', *Research on Social Work Practice*, vol.3, no.20, pp. 208–218

Markus, G. (1979) *Analyzing Panel Data*, Sage, Beverly Hills

Menard, S. (1991) *Longitudinal Research*, Sage, Beverly Hills

Miles, M. (1979) 'Qualitative data as an attractive nuisance: The problem of analysis', *Administrative Science Quarterly*, vol.24, no.4, pp. 590–601

O'Connor, I., Dalgleish, L. & Khan, J. (1984) 'A reflection of the rising spectre of conservatism: The fate of personal models of social work in beginning practice', *British Journal of Social Work*, vol.14, pp. 227–240

Plewis, I. (1985) *Analyzing Change: Measurement and Explanation Using Longitudinal Data*, Wiley, Chichester

Poulin, J. & Walter, C. (1993) 'Social worker burnout', *Social Work Research and Abstracts*, vol.29, no.4, pp. 5–11

Roberts, J. (1985) *Successful Submission Writing*, Information Australia, Melbourne

Ryan, M., Fook, J. & Hawkins, L. (1995) 'From beginner to graduate social worker: Preliminary findings of an Australian longitudinal study', *British Journal of Social Work*, vol.25, no.1, pp. 17–35

Schon, D. (1983) *The Reflective Practitioner*, Basic Books, New York

Secker, J. (1993) *From Theory to Practice in Social Work: The Development of Social Work Students' Practice*, Avebury, Aldershot

Part IV

Developing practice theory

11 Theorising as research: Developing a theory of radical casework practice
Jan Fook

The premise that we have accepted in this book is that formal theory need not be privileged over practice experience. This chapter gives an account of research which makes the opposite assumption. It is the story of research which was based on the idea that general theory can be used in a deductive manner to inform specific practice. It is my story of how I developed a theory of radical casework practice.

WHY DO THE RESEARCH?

Like many ordinary people, I suppose, I began my research for mainly circumstantial reasons. I had just gained my first academic position, and was encouraged to obtain a higher degree. I had studied undergraduate social work in the mid-1970s, when casework was beginning to be unfashionable, but my staunch interest in individual work remained intact during my four years of study. In my new job I taught about the welfare state. In preparing my early lectures, I looked again at radical critiques of social work, and became fascinated with the question of where this left the possibility of radical casework practice. So, given the professional motivation to do postgraduate research work, and a sufficiently interesting intellectual problem to explore, I glibly enrolled in a Master of Social Work program at the University of Sydney at the beginning of 1981.

I finally submitted my research thesis in the middle of 1986. I am fond of saying, even now, that if I had known beforehand what was involved I would never have undertaken the work. In hindsight, I probably would have, but restatement of this idea at least allows me the comfort of expressing some little of the intellectual and emotional trauma I experienced. I do not mean to suggest that I believe my experience is unique, or that anyone could have or should have prepared me for the difficulties I was to encounter. I simply believe that acknowledging the personal struggles that contribute to a piece of research normalises the experience for others and gives some context to the research act.

BEGINNING THE RESEARCH AND REVIEWING THE LITERATURE

The first year of the research process felt shamefully easy. I had a vague idea that what I was engaged in was called a 'literature review', but apart from doing lots of reading, and jotting down the odd idea, I had no articulate notion of where I was heading, or even what I should be aiming for. It was after reading in this unstructured fashion for about a year, and experiencing the frustration of wasting time chasing up references which I discovered I had already read, that I realised it might be sensible to systematise my work in some way. So I began to meticulously record the publishing details of every piece of work I read, but also to make my notes in a form which allowed me to cross-reference ideas and arguments more easily. I found it helpful to make a short summary (of no more than 100 words) of the main argument of the work so that I could gain, in little more than a glance, the gist of it. The rest of my notes, also succinct, consisted of my comments and critique on the ideas I felt might be useful for later reference. I found the discipline of having to condense the main argument and value of a work into a few sentences very helpful in focusing my own thinking.

As it happened, this way of summarising, classifying and analysing the literature was very beneficial in allowing me to distil the general trends, and to identify any gaps which needed more work. This, I discovered later, is the stated purpose of a literature review. However, I also found that a comprehensive reading and understanding of the literature is of course beneficial in meeting one of the more hidden agendas, in that any 'academic' or 'scientific' piece of research must demonstrate knowledge of relevant literature.

Defining the limits of what I read felt like a more or less arbitrary decision. Clearly I needed to be familiar with any literature which talked about 'radical' social work, but exactly how this was defined was, it goes without saying, problematic. I ended up reading anything I could on Marxist, socialist, structural social work, and then, since time did not stand still while I was doing my research, had to expand this to include the newer feminist writings as they emerged. In a way I had to make a decision about the boundaries of radical social work before I felt I had read enough and before I felt confident enough to define it clearly for myself. This process of having to gain, as it were, a qualitative overview of an area, before feeling that you have the definitive knowledge, is a constant tension in any form of research, I think. There is a continual movement between developing a 'hunch', further investigation, modifying or changing the hunch, and so on. In retrospect, this differs little from the processes involved in addressing practice situations—making tentative interpretations, gaining more information, changing and developing the interpretations, and so on. Rowan, as quoted by Reason (1988, p.7) gives a nice description of this process and the tensions involved as they are often experienced when undertaking research:

> Ideas start churning around. THINKING in this model is not the application of a technnique to inert material—it is a creative process of innovation and testing. It continually asks the question—'Will this Do?' . . . the major contradiction here is between always needing more information ('Maybe that new paper will have the answer') and feeling that there is too much information already, and [it] needs to be cut down. It is only when this contradiction is transcended that movement takes place to the next stage.

After a couple of years spent mainly reading and taking systematic notes, I felt confident enough to categorise the trends in the literature. At that time there seemed to be about four different types of literature which related to radical social work: 1) works which were primarily critiques of the professions, social work included; 2) works which were mainly criticisms of casework; 3) literature which outlined radical theory and developed the implications for practice (mainly collective strategies); and 4) literature which argued the importance of a radical casework. Of course what was missing became glaringly obvious: there was almost *no* literature which developed what radical casework would look like in concrete practice.

I was happy because the original research problem with which I had begun my search remained intact. It seemed to me that it should be a relatively easy task to ask why this was the case, and to design a piece of research to investigate this problem.

FORMULATING THE RESEARCH QUESTION

Apart from the usual pragmatic difficulties of juggling work, study and home life, the other main problem was primarily an intellectual one. I was constantly becoming confused about how to frame what I wanted to work on. I knew I wanted to work on radical casework, and my extensive reading to this point had only strengthened my commitment—that was not the issue. But how was I to frame this as a research problem, and why did the specifics of it keep changing with everything new I read? For instance, I unearthed so many issues that were tied up with radical casework—the need to connect personal problems with social structures, the need to integrate broad theory and analysis, the difference between casework and counselling, the nature of social work—the list became mind boggling. I somehow had to address all these issues yet keep my topic manageable and focused enough. Other issues concerned me as well. I became pre-occupied with the idea that whatever I chose to do would have to be presented and justified in such a form as to pass examination as an academic thesis. The easist way to ensure this is to choose the narrowest possible area, so that I could feel confident I had done it justice. On the other hand, I really wanted to work on a problem to which I felt I could make a major contribution. I only wanted to work on something I believed in. To complicate matters, I thought that enough radical critiques of casework existed—I actually wanted to *do* something with the ideas so that they could have some direct practical application, not just map out the problem further. So for me the intellectual struggle became emotional and existential as well.

In the end I found a pragmatic solution to the problem. The best way for me to keep a lid on all the angst and confusion was to write down what I thought my main research problems and questions were, and the sub-problems and questions, and to keep referring to this every time I read something which prompted my thinking in another direction. It would then be a simple matter of relating that new idea back to my original questions. I actually kept these on a card in the front of the card file which contained all my notes on the references I'd read. That way I could look at it whenever I made a new addition to the file. It sounds trite in hindsight, but I discovered that the only way for me to keep making sense of all my ideas and not become overwhelmed was to keep categorising, ordering and prioritising my ideas into main points, sub-points and related points. I am sure there are many people who are not fazed by complexity and can easily maintain their intellectual focus. I was not one of them. I had to rely on some pretty simple structuring to see me through the design stages of my research work. But the very simplicity of my research question, 'What is radical casework?', and the clear problems I wanted to address (showing that the practice of radical casework could exist in theory, and what this theory of practice could look like) belie the tedious hours involved in distilling complex ideas into this short clear form.

DESIGNING THE RESEARCH

I suspect that designing theoretical research is much more difficult than designing empirical work, since with empirical work there are known and accepted structures in which to present work. Theoretical work can conceivably be presented in any way that is convincing. Although I had studied research methods twice before undertaking my own research, neither of the courses satisfactorily covered anything as mundane as research design and thesis organisation. As well, I did not feel confident enough to construct my own design—I was too worried about passing the examination process for that. In the end I was provided with some structure by a sympathetic colleague and friend who was familiar with my constant struggles. He showed me the standard format for the presentation of empirical research results (literature review, theoretical framework, design and methods, results, discussion and future directions). I simply modified this to suit my topic, and I was on my way with an outer framework. The literature review became my chapters arguing for a theory of radical casework practice, showing a need for radical casework and that it was not necessarily discounted by radical criticism, and then showing how current literature did not address the issue adequately. I built up my theoretical framework from the literature, showing what sorts of requirements a successful theory of radical casework practice would need to fulfil. My 'methods' section was to be a chapter on my framework for presenting this theory of practice, including a definition of terms, and the 'results' section was in fact my detailed presentation of this framework. All I needed now was to fill in some of the details.

It was not until this stage that I committed myself to a solely theoretical piece of work. I had been open all along to the possibility of undertaking an empirical study, but once I had formulated my research question I became convinced that I could not design a sound empirical study of radical casework without first delineating what it should look like from the literature. This of course was a big enough task in itself, so my thesis became a theoretical one. I then simply had to decide what would be the most convincing way to present my theory of radical casework practice.

As usual, this proved to be a much more difficult task than I imagined. I had become so used to blithely exhorting my students to apply theory to practice that I presumed it would be as easy for me to do as them! When I sat down to the task of applying Marxist analysis to personal problems, I began to appreciate why not much had been written on radical casework! At first I decided that what was needed was a better theory to connect individual and social structure, read Peter Leonard's excellent book *Ideology and Personality* (1984), and became confused again. I was just heading off to read Bourdieu, as recommended by some sociologist friends, when it suddenly struck me that the Marxist concept of ideology, coupled with feminist ideas around self-defeating beliefs internalised by women, was really enough of a starting point. This was after all a *social work* thesis, and what I should be doing was writing about *social work*. I did not deny the use and value of extensive social theories, but to my way of thinking, these were for the social theorists to develop. And if I, as a social work researcher, was not going to devote myself to developing social work theory, then who was?

This latter thought was one of the most liberating I had in the course of my thesis research—indeed, one of the most liberating in the course of my whole career so far. It stopped me trying to emulate academics from other disciplines and gave me pride and sense of purpose in what I could and should contribute to the profession as a social work academic. Incidentally, it sent me back to social work literature and what it had to say about theory and practice. I decided to frame my work in the same ways that social work practice theory was traditionally presented. I felt this would make it easier for social workers to connect with, but it also seemed a helpful way to formulate practice theory. Thus it was that I looked at all the major works on social-work-practice theory models—Hollis (1964), Perlman (1957), Roberts and Nee (1970), Turner (1986) Compton and Galaway (1989)—and distilled the major elements I thought needed to be developed in a model of practice—theoretical assumptions, social work assessment, goals and methods/practice strategies. It only remained now to fill in the details.

APPLYING THEORY TO PRACTICE

Having the framework is not the same as having the techniques. In the end, I relied primarily on logic and imagination. I simply described a particular theoretical concept (for example, 'ideology'), and then thought about what type of problem assessment, social work goals, and practice strategies might be logically suggested by it. In the case of the concept of ideology (the idea that the personal consciousness of individual people is at least partly formed by the social structure, and that they thus hold internalised beliefs which support the status quo), it was easy to see that this gave a logical point at which personal problems might emerge—from holding internalised beliefs which might in fact be contrary to the well-being of that person. The logical focus of assistance is thus these beliefs. It only remains to use and develop practice strategies which expose, challenge and change these beliefs.

To develop practice strategies, I turned in the first instance to existing literature and asked myself how traditional techniques (such as counselling, interpersonal skills) might need to be modified, changed or expanded to achieve the aims of radical casework. In some cases it was simply a mater of reporting and reviewing literature which already attempted to do this. In other cases, I needed to apply a critique of a particular skill before developing a new formulation. Sometimes I asked myself what unintended effects the use of a particular skill or strategy might have, and if 'non-radical' outcomes were possible, I reformulated the strategy so as to minimise them.

Another technique was to ask myself: If I assumed the existence of ideology, how would this affect my own behaviour and practices, and that of my clients and colleagues, as well as the situations in which we found ourselves? Which of my own beliefs and behaviours might perform 'ideological' functions, and how would awareness of this change my behaviour and attitudes?

So it was that the intellectual task of applying theory to practice became a simple matter of gleaning relevant theoretical concepts from the literature, then deductively applying each one by asking how an awareness of each concept would change my analysis of a situation, my goals for casework assistance, and my actual practices. The processes involved were clearly reducible to asking particular questions of my material in order to derive particular sorts of answers. For example, I asked myself specific questions about skills, if I wanted to derive a specific skill. (Le Croy, 1990, p.263 gives some useful pointers about asking different types of questions in order to seek different types of knowledge.) In this way I built up a theory of radical casework practice.

With this structure, it was actually a relatively easy task to finish writing the thesis. Over the four and a half years I worked on the thesis, two were spent solely in reading and thinking, the next year yielded only two chapters (heavily theoretical ones), and the final year yielded the remaining eight. I spent an entire six months in revisions (without a word processor). The thesis was published, with some substantial changes and new chapters, at the end of 1992 (Fook, 1993).

REFLECTING ON MY ACCOUNT

In writing my account, I tried to follow the guidelines I described in

Chapter 1. What you have just read is therefore my attempt to construct as clearly as possible my experience in concrete and specific terms, including my reflections where I believe they are integral to my account. What follows is my more detailed reflection on my account itself.

On re-reading my account, I am struck by my preoccupation with structure. It is probably a little unfair to analyse work from the 1980s in the post-structuralist light of the 1990s, but the language I use in my account—'clarity', 'simplicity', 'confusion', 'systematising', 'argue'—does seem to indicate a concern with certainty, with being able to control and master by reason the many ideas which came crowding in upon me. I make no apology for this, but I do admit that the account is one of a very scientific model—hierarchical and linear, moving logically from cause to effect.

It is also an account which emphasises difficulty, pain and struggle rather than ease, satisfaction or enjoyment. I seem to hold an implicit assumption that the task *has* to be difficult. I gloss over the periods when the work becomes easy (in the final year of writing), and I am even 'ashamed' that the first year of reading was 'easy'. I mention only once that I was happy, and this was only because I didn't have to change my research problem! I wonder where these assumptions came from? I guess I held implicit assumptions about research—that it was necessarily scientific and systematic (this distinguished it from mere subjective experience) and, because it was removed from personal experience, must necessarily be hard. It seems too easy to dismiss these as merely the assumptions of the dominant masculinist academic culture which I had unconsciously assumed. They were, but it was also the only academic culture I knew, and I did embrace them as very much my own assumptions at the time. They also bespeak a well-entrenched Protestant work ethic, which was also an integral part of my social background. There was no gap between my 'espoused theory' and my 'theory in use' on this score.

I suspect that emphasising the pain, difficulty, and 'lonesome struggle' nature of the work also performs the function of increasing its value. 'The work must be good if it was so hard to do'—how often do I hear this lament from students? 'I should have gained a good mark because I put so much work into it.' How often have I challenged with my students the assumption that hard work necessarily results in good work. It is sobering for me to recognise that this very premise characterises the way I see my own work.

One of the overriding themes I see in my account is a picture of the research as being very much conducted solely within the parameters of my own head. What seems to be missing is an account of the role other people played, and how interactions with other people might have influenced my work. It is hard to know how much of this is my chosen interpretation of my experience, or whether this reflects my actual behaviour at the time, or whether it even matters. Certainly I seem to assume that the task must necessarily be a solitary one in the same way it must necessarily be a difficult one. What intrigues me is that I can and do recall many instances when I whinged, raged, complained, appealed and cried to friends, supervisors and colleagues. What I do not remember is ever expecting that these behaviours would help me achieve the goal of actually completing the research (even though I must emphatically acknowledge in hindsight that they did, as did the patience of my associates). I also must acknowledge that upon reflection I am extremely grateful for the support and assistance of these various people. Somehow, however, I saw the task as my sole responsibility.

I recall one occasion in particular when I felt almost overwhelmed by the difficulty of it all. I was struggling to write a chapter which argued for the radical potential of casework. I had spent months on the specific thinking and planning, but found that the writing itself would still not come easily. I had spent two whole days trying to write the introduction to the chapter. My grandmother, to whom I had been especially attached, had died unexpectedly the night before. Nothing I wrote made any sense. In desperation I phoned my superviser, who hastened to assure me that it was quite acceptable to take this long to write a chapter. I don't think I even told my supervisor of my grandmother's death. I presented it as a purely academic problem. This underscores for me the notion that I must have seen the research and thesis writing as an essentially independent and intellectual experience. This is borne out by another gap in my account. Although I allude in the beginning to the *emotional* trauma I experienced, the account is almost solely about *intellectual* struggle. The more personal and emotional aspects of my experience are kept peripheral in my account. Perhaps another reason for this is the fact that I did not expect my work to be so difficult intellectually. This is related to another of my assumptions, I think: I believed at the outset that I was capable of the task intellectually, hence it was the unexpected trauma of this side of the work which caused me most heartache.

As I re-read my account, I ask myself how *I* personally influenced the research process. I wonder if it was my own confidence in the power of the intellect which led me to construct my account in more intellectual terms? On the other hand, I do seem to have left out many aspects of the experience which I know were important to me—the joy of learning, the increased confidence in developing new skills, the passion for research, the satisfaction of producing ideas in which I believed. At the time I loved (and still do) academic pursuits—study, debate, creating new ideas and challenging old ones.

I cherished (and still do) the opportunity to express *my* ideas in *my* way. Raised in a fundamentalist Protestant family, I have reacted by making independence of thinking somewhat of an article of faith. I therefore experienced my research primarily as a *liberating* experience. So despite the fact that I adopted potentially dis-affirming individualist and rationalist assumptions, and a potentially rigid scientific model, my overall experience of undertaking the research was actually affirming and strengthening. I think this is why I might have been determined to maintain the belief that it was I who must achieve the work independently—it was important for me to feel that the work was mine, and therein lay a great deal of my personal satisfaction. This serves as a reminder to me that experience also needs to be interpreted relative to personal background. The personal meaning of a situation might be quite different from our stereotyped assumptions about its political correctness or otherwise.

Another pattern I notice in the account is the sense of successive hurdles encountered and surmounted. The need and use of structure is paramount in my account, and structure (and the associated rational techniques) is used mainly to surmount the hurdles—I use structured frameworks and systems to organise my thoughts, to help me see relationships between ideas, and to communicate and express my ideas. It seems, however, to be an entirely different set of skills or circumstances that actually shows me what and where the hurdles are—I either get the frameworks themselves, or redirect myself, through the chance assistance of other people (getting a framework for the reporting of empirical research from a colleague) or through the seemingly chance intuitive connection (the sudden realisation of what I thought the role of social work researchers should be).

DEVELOPING MY THEORY AND PRACTICE

In general, I do not think my espoused theory of how to conduct research was very different from the assumptions implicit in what I actually did. Although the work was not empirical, I enacted it on broadly positivist assumptions which were congruent with the way I believed (at the time) research ought to be conducted. What was possibly incongruent in hindsight was the type of methodology with the subject matter and aims of the research. If I were to undertake the research again now, I would not forgo the painstaking thinking involved in clarifying my theory of radical casework practice. But I would be interested in employing other, perhaps more action-oriented designs to complement the purely intellectual exercise. In Chapters 12 and 13, Margaret Lynn and Ann Ingamells talk about their research projects, in which they use these sorts of methods to develop practice theory.

In retrospect it is tempting to be more critical of my structured format and methods than I think the period and context in which I undertook the research warrant. I am almost embarrassed by the certain and sometimes overly simplistic way in which my work is presented. John Drayton (1994) encapsulates eloquently and fairly many of the criticisms I would now make. Does this mean I would conduct the work any differently if I were to undertake it now?

This is a question I have been asking myself intermittently over the last decade, and it is intertwined with the question of how I see the importance and use of structure. I know it is fashionable now to decry the imposition of certainty and unity, but I can only say, from my experience in writing *Radical Casework*, that I believe that task would have been impossible without it. I do not argue that I could not have produced another, probably better type of work with a different type of methodology, but that the work as it stands holds meaning for me, and, as I have been told, for some practitioners and students as well. It seems that there are still some of us who appreciate structure, simplicity and clarity! My account of the research experience of constructing my theory, however, reminded me of the judicious interplay of structure and technique, chance encounter and intuitive flash which characterised the research process for me. In comparing this with my subsequent research experiences, I can only say the parallels continue. I believe it is important therefore to be able to combine the use of structure and rational, often mundane technique with the (perhaps more creative) insights afforded by less structured and routinised thinking. (Wood, 1990, pp. 384–385, gives some pointers as to how to combine the two types of thinking.)

Unfortunately, in trying to communicate and teach people how to try to arrive at these insights, there is a risk of reducing what is often an intuitive process to a series of mechanistic techniques. (This is the same dilemma faced in giving any work a structure—you immediately discount the possibility of other forms.) I turned, therefore, to authors more experienced at this than I—both C. Wright Mills (1959), in his chapter on intellectual craftsmanship, and Weissman (1990) suggest some helpful techniques and circumstances to stimulate creative thinking.

The issue of how to work with and use structure without it dominating a situation remains a question in my teaching as well as my research practice. My main area of teaching is social work practice, and I constantly resist students' demands to 'tell us what to do'. I firmly believe that it is best for students to learn how to work out what to do for themselves, yet this reply often sounds like a 'cop-out' to beginning students who do not feel they know where to start. Unfortunately it also becomes somewhat of an excuse for lecturers to simply teach unadulterated theory ungrounded in practice. My task, therefore, becomes one of trying to teach students how to work out what to do, using practice experience, but without allowing concrete practices to preclude the development of fluid ways of thinking and action. Here again the dilemma rears its ugly head. It is difficult to teach the 'how to' to a group of novices without over-simplifying the process, yet beginning students often ask for a simplified, concrete structure which allows them to connect with the material. On the other hand, teaching with too much structure often does not allow the 'spirit' of social work to come through as one needs to experience it in order to practise responsively, and it may pre-empt personal efforts to engage with a problem. In my uncertainty on this issue, I was most heartened to read, in Belenky *et al.*'s famous study of how women learn (1986), that many women found a degree of structure helpful and often felt that they floundered or wasted time without it. I guess I now feel empowered to use structure in my service and not to fear that it must necessarily commandeer my creativity or the more uncertain aspects of my work. I do not feel fearful of it, or apologetic—I use it for what service it does me. *I* am in control.

In some ways this encapsulates the way I now feel about theory. I have always loved theorising. That has not changed, and that is just a personal quirk of mine. Before I began the research I think I was a little mystified, a little charmed, and a little alarmed by it. I think there is a tendency in social work to accord too much status to theory. Doing my research allowed me to confront the beast THEORY full on and live to tell the tale. I now still feel charmed by it, but not mystified or alarmed. I believe I can now see theory as a construction of mine which I use differently in different contexts— as a stimulus to thinking and practice; as a tool to conceptualise and develop practice; as a discourse framework with which to communicate about practice; as a basis from which to criticise and develop practice; as a way of understanding practice; and sometimes as a structure to guide our practice in uncertain situations. Dennis Saleebey (1993) differentiates usefully between the last usage (which he would call 'normative' theory), and the more 'generative' possibilities of theorising suggested by some of the former. I agree with him that 'theories which translate social science theories for employment in social work practice' are precious little (p.10). It was working on *Radical Casework* that made clear to me that this was where I wanted to make my contribution in social work. I no longer feel I have to apologise for being an academic to social work practitioners, nor do I have to be embarrassed as a social worker when I am with other academics. I have a vision for the place of theory in social work, and I am happy that my work is to help in carving this out.

REFERENCES

Belenky, M., Clinchy, B., Goldberger, N. & Tarule, J. (1986) *Women's Ways of Knowing*, Basic Books/Harper Collins, New York

Compton, B. & Galaway, B. (1989) *Social Work Processes*, Dorsey, Illinois

Drayton, J. (1994) Book review of *Radical Casework: A Theory of Practice*, *Australian Social Work*, vol. 47, no. 4, pp.56–57

Fook, J. (1993) *Radical Casework: A Theory of Practice*, Allen & Unwin, Sydney

Hollis, F. (1964) *Casework: A Psychosocial Therapy*, Random House, New York

Le Croy, C.W. (1990) 'Opening the door to knowledge utilization', in Videka-Sherman, L. & Reid, W.J. (eds) *Advances in Clinical Social Work Research*, National Association of Social Workers, Silver Spring, pp. 261–264

Leonard, P. (1984) *Ideology and Personality*, Macmillan, London

Mills, C. W. (1970) *The Sociological Imagination*, Penguin, Harmondsworth

Perlman, H. H. (1957) *Casework: A Problem-Solving Process*, University of Chicago Press, Chicago & London

Roberts, R. & Nee, R.H. (1970) *Theories of Social Casework*, University of Chicago Press, Chicago & London

Reason, P. (ed.) (1988) *Human Inquiry in Action*, Sage, London

Turner, F. (1986) *Social Work Treatment*, Free Press, New York

Weissman, H. (ed.) (1990) *Serious Play: Creativity and Innovation in Social Work*, National Association of Social Workers, Silver Springs

Wood, K. (1990) 'Epistemological issues in the development of social work practice knowledge', in Videka-Sherman, L. & Reid, W. J. (eds) *Advances in Clinical Social Work Research*, NASW, Silver Spring, pp. 373–390

12 Negotiating practice theory (or, I've got the theory, you've got the practice)
Marg Lynn

The research discussed in this chapter grew from my belief that rural social work practice should be different from metropolitan practice because it needs to reflect the culture and environment of rural people. While much of the literature prescribes the need for a different rural paradigm and practice (for example, Martinez-Brawley, 1985), other literature disputes the existence of such a specialty (for example, York, Denton & Moran, 1989), or indicates that it is the exception rather than the rule in rural practice (Wharf, 1984). Very little of this practice has been described and evaluated to demonstrate how it has been adapted to fit with its environment, in order to offer the greatest value to its constituency.

My previous experience in rural social work practice, and my observations of others' practice, gave me concern about the possibility of social workers ignoring major aspects of the rural cultural context. For example, it is part of the 'common wisdom' that informal networks are highly significant in rural areas and are depended on more than in metropolitan areas. I suspected that they were frequently overlooked by social workers, leading to partial or complete duplication of existing supportive networks by professionalised services or processes, which may not be as relevant or acceptable.

My concern was to conceptualise a form of rural practice that was progressive, empowering, and congruent with the rural culture and environment. I wanted to develop an approach which did more than merely reflect the conservatism inherent in much remedial social work thinking, in much of the community care ideology, and in much of rural community life. (I am aware that there are already some inherent contradictions in these aims.)

CHOICE OF METHODOLOGY

I wanted to interview a small number of experienced practitioners in my region to explore with them the nature of their relationships with informal networks. However, after substantial reading of the rural social work literature I was caught in a dilemma between, on the one hand, wanting to gain insight into workers' practice and, on the other, wanting to share with them the wisdom of others which could inform their work.

I therefore decided to develop a model of practice. I would expose it to the critical comment of those best able both to decide how congruent it might be with current rural practice and to indicate whether it might enhance practice. The process was aimed at ensuring that the model reflected practice realities rather than being purely a theoretical exercise. It was a way of maximising the benefits of sharing my knowledge, and acquiring some of the participants' knowledge, and in the process negotiating a new form of practice. While my reading had helped me make much greater sense of my own past practice in the rural social work field, I could not assume that others were either unaware of this knowledge or would be attracted to the ideological underpinning of my interpretation of it. I needed therefore to establish a baseline by first asking workers to talk about their practice. Second, I explored what they thought of the way I had conceptualised practice to see how much common ground we could establish and codify.

This unfolding methodology was essentially qualitative. Solely gathering information about their practice would have lent itself to either a quantitative approach, to verify assumptions, or a qualitative approach, to explore the nature of their relationships with networks, integrated with my interpretation in the light of the literature. Solely offering knowledge to the field (in a researchable form such as a model) would have involved possibly erroneous assumptions that I recognised a need for a new paradigm and practice and workers did not. Other methods were rejected as unsuitable.

A quantitative approach is used for verification, and assumes that the parameters are known and the focus is partialised and measurable. It offers little scope for opening up the practitioners' experience for greater understanding. Such an approach could have established more knowledge about known variables but would be unhelpful in establishing what these variables were. In asking respondents to discuss how they conceptualised rural practice, I made no assumptions about the nature of this practice, other than that it is different from metropolitan practice—though they could have refuted that too if they wished.

A collaborative approach, while also lending itself to qualitative methods, was also rejected on the ground that it required more time than I had available. Collaborative research assumes a shared investment in the outcomes by researcher and participants, and a joint exploration of the issues raised. It also requires a collaborative development of all parts of the research, including defining the research question and the methodology (Pease, 1987; 1990). I did not at the time entirely think through the collaborative process I might have adopted. However, a substantial number of meetings with the individual participants or, more appropriately, a number of group meetings would have been required—to develop a collaborative climate, to share what I had learnt from my review of the literature, and to explore the depth of understanding and range of perspectives in the group on how they conceptualised the field. Consensus might then have been sought on what we saw as exciting research challenges, and to which they and I could commit ourselves. Collaborative approaches would hence have demanded a much more open-ended timetable, both to meet the time demands of several others, and because the research might have led in unpredictable directions. As it was, interviews to explore their practice and the congruency of the model with it were containable in the limited time I set myself to complete the research.

The research therefore took the form of my shaping a practice model, out of my blend of the literature on both rural social work and social support networks, and asking respondents to reflect on it. Discussion of the model was preceded by a number of open-ended questions about their practice experience and conceptualising of rurality and rural practice. Social workers were selected who had been in their current position for at least two years in a rural, not provincial area of Gippsland, and who together represented a range of agency types. Once they had agreed to participate, I sent them a precis of the model to contemplate before the interview. Interviews lasted about two hours.

As indicated, I believed that the aims of this research were best served by a qualitative approach. Cook and Reichardt (1977) describe the qualitative paradigm as 'phenomenological, inductive, subjective, holistic, process-oriented and holding a socio-anthropological world view'. These attributes of the method can be demonstrated in the research.

Participants were asked to describe the world of their practice as they experienced it. They were asked to start with their experience and relate it to the model or concepts within it, not vice versa. It was the whole, not fragments of their experience, that they brought into their discussion. The research interaction aimed to elicit something of how they experienced their work: what they enjoyed, what was important to them. I was interested in the process by which they engaged with their community, as much as in their achievements. Finally, the assumptions underscoring the interaction of all participants in the research were founded on beliefs about the need to understand the social system in its diverse cultural forms as a basis for planning and implementing appropriate intervention strategies.

The model was presented to participants for discussion, and for comparing and contrasting against their reality of practice. Both the model and practice were exposed to examination. Deductively, the model was tested against their reality. Inductively, participants could explore and describe their practice as currently conceptualised.

When I had nearly completed writing up the thesis for which this research journey was undertaken, I travelled (physically) to some of the remoter, sparsely populated parts of Australia. I wanted to get a sense of the applicability of what I had been writing about, in areas both distant and different from my home region of Gippsland. Gippsland is a large region of Victoria whose economy is based predominantly in the south on the dairying industry, in the centre on energy production from coal and oil, and in the east on timber and mixed farming. My respondents were spread across the region. The closest to Melbourne, the capital city, was 130 kilometres away, the furthest, 330 km.

My experiences provided me with both a clearer vision and a metaphor for what I had been exploring. It demonstrated for me the inescapable need for a qualitative approach. On my return I wrote:

> There is little empirical research in rural social work and hence there is little documentation and codification of rural practice, especially in Australia. Few landmarks are fixed. The territory needs to be mapped, the texture of the terrain described, the features identified and named, waterholes found and sites for artesian bores located, routes worked out and appropriate vehicles designed, tested and acquired. In order for social work to avoid becoming an imperialist invasion of the rural environment, the local culture must be understood and respected, the language learnt and the benefits negotiated with the local communities.
>
> My research forms part of the basic mapping of the territory, as well as some design and testing of an appropriate vehicle, and as such it needs to be both exploratory and qualitative in approach. (Lynn, 1990, p.38–39)

NEGOTIATING KNOWLEDGE AND RESOLVING TENSIONS

This research can be usefully viewed as a process of negotiations in resolving dilemmas, tensions, contradictions or potential conflicts of interest, both in the content and in the method of research. However, writing about the research has involved confronting further dilemmas that have appeared under retrospective scrutiny.

Model building itself began as my own compromise between 'telling and asking'. My hope in developing a provisional model was that together we, the research participants and myself, would frame and codify a new paradigm, thereby negotiating new and useful knowledge. The outcomes were more humble. The exploration of practice was mutually stimulating, with participants expressing interest in the process and enjoying the opportunity afforded to examine their work from a new perspective. They confirmed that rural practice is different. However, it became apparent that accepting that a model had validity was different from accepting that it could or would be implemented.

The enduring methodological tension arising from the research is that the model was presented as a holistic approach to rural practice, whereas the respondents preferred to see it as one more approach to use selectively and partially. This is consistent with the findings of research (for example, Carew, 1979) that suggests that social workers do not specifically and consciously use theory and, further (Bailey & Lee 1982; Hardiker & Barker, 1981), that they do not use a single model but draw selectively (and usually unconsciously) from multiple sources. A few contemporary examples would suggest that this need not be the case where programs have been established on the basis of theoretical models rather than a more pragmatic response to need. Family group conferencing, intensive homemaker services and child abuse treatment programs are such examples. I am optimistic that this rural social work practice model could have some currency holistically. Action research is required to implement and evaluate it.

On reflection, it was the unnegotiated aspects that finally carried more weight in determining the immediate outcomes of the research. I have indicated that I approached experienced social workers in my area, most of whom I knew previously. Perhaps because of this, their willing involvement was also accompanied by a sense of doing me a favour. But the research was not collaborative. My preliminary contact with them raised interest but not a sense of ownership, and hence no commitment was established then or later to invest in the outcome by testing the model holistically. (It was never my *intention* to test it during this research process. However, in retrospect, I recognise that I had hoped, or perhaps even assumed, that my participants would find the material as fascinating as I did, and would find trialling it irresistible!)

My own methodology therefore contradicted the substance of the practice model itself, which aimed at community empowerment through processes of facilitating local ownership, consciousness raising and political action. I had side-stepped the fundamental processes I otherwise espoused. I had ignored the necessary parallels between researcher and respondent, and social worker and client/community. My espoused preference, to further the analogy, would be to treat all clients like research collaborators, rather than to treat research respondents like clients. Practice should vest as much ownership as possible in those whose experiences it concerns. Respondents and clients will both resist prescriptive approaches. In exercising a 'theory in use' at variance with my 'espoused theory', I introduced a tension into the process, of which I was not conscious at the time.

The continuing subtext of the research was a quest for synthesis. Social work poses constant challenges to find a balance between competing principles and to establish the common ground between polarities. (Social care and social control are common examples.) Methodologically and theoretically, the research produced tensions requiring resolution or reconciliation.

My initial methodological dilemma between asking and telling was resolved by the development of the model, though I now believe a more complete resolution of this tension might have been the development of a collaborative approach. The theoretical content of the model was similarly full of the contradictions and tensions that constantly challenge practice. The model used a framework of ideas drawn from the work of Emelia Martinez-Brawley, a prolific contributor to the American rural social work literature. Each of her tenets can be seen as raising substantial dilemmas. How does a practitioner in a conservative rural community reconcile encouraging local decision making and problem ownership with the risk of co-option of the processes by powerful people whose values are antithetical to social justice principles? How does effective practice, built on a partnership with informal networks, avoid getting hijacked as cheap practice? How does a practitioner work to build coalitions of interest that are sufficiently strong to support sometimes conflictual political action, in a usually consensus-oriented and conflict-suppressing community?

These questions embody core contradictions within Martinez-Brawley's concepts of indigenisation, conscientisation and politicisation (1980) which my research highlighted. Both research and practice need to recognise the contradictions and not align themselves exclusively with one side of the duality. Observing the dynamic tension is necessary to keep in touch with each side and not alienate potential contributors to the discourse. In this way, values may be negotiated and the agenda widened from the narrower concerns of traditional local politics, to include a broader social justice perspective.

The political aspect of the model emphasises the reality that understanding and respecting a local culture are bound by considerations of time and place. It also has considerable significance in relation to the meaning of social work. Community and state politics have changed dramatically in Victoria since I undertook my research, (a languishing Labor government was replaced in October 1992 by a Liberal (conservative) government which proceeded to dismantle much of the publicly owned infrastructure and abandon community consultative processes). The relative complacency with which politics was viewed at the time of my research had implications for how the political content of the model was perceived. Arguably, the role of the state has changed since then in Victoria to that of radical change agent. This shift would appear to give support to social work's strengthening its role as an agent of balance and synthesis. Building coalitions across a range of interest groups and political perspectives is part of the practice model's content. Building intellectual bridges that facilitate communication and create greater understanding of community needs and unrepresented perspectives is the challenge which both allies social work with other professions and marks its special contribution. But sadly and ironically, working for change under an economic rationalist government substantially involves working to restore the status quo rather than to transform social institutions in line with a more socially just agenda.

All respondents were comfortable with the political nature of the model, which involved working with informal networks using processes of consciousness raising about the causes of rural community powerlessness. Nonetheless, some interpreted it according to their own level of current political commitment. I would speculate now, without any disrespect, that their 'espoused theory' of political analysis would be more radical and their 'theory in use' more conservative.

An unresolved tension remains concerning the degree of legitimate politicisation of social work. My model requires a high degree of political consciousness and activity. Accepting it holistically, and therefore acknowledging the interconnectedness of all issues and processes in the rural environment, would imply an acceptance by social work of such a political role. How different can social work become and still remain social work?

MODELS OF KNOWING

The inseparability of the knower and the known, the subject and the object, has become a truism in non-positivist research. The choice of methodology sometimes says as much about the researcher as it does about the subject matter. It is only in reflecting on the process for the purpose of writing this chapter that I have realised how true this is. I had chosen to develop a model to present to my respondents, and, as I saw it at the time, this was in order to establish a reciprocal, non-exploitative relationship with workers in the field. A model offered something tangible to relate to and argue for, against, or around. It did not require them to establish their own context, and it allowed a structure for analysis and for the development of new practice.

I now realise that I also developed a model in this form because it is a means of communication that is compatible with my normal *modus operandi* and interpersonal comfort level. I prefer to have thought through my position, at least provisionally, before exposing it to public inspection. I would have been less productive in a more spontaneous dialogue about practice. The model reflected my processes, providing me with a research tool that was an expression of my cognitive and interpersonal style.

The model also reflected my values in the way in which I had selected knowledge to build the theoretical framework. The literature review which provided the foundation for the model had been shaped and filtered through my experience, my values, my interpretation and my theorising.

My practice model became both the vehicle and the destination, or the subject and the object, of the research. Its tangibility merged with the intangibility of my model of knowing (in Schon's term). Schon suggests that professionals have an implicit model of practice in which they 'know more than they can say', using Polanyi's notion of tacit knowledge (Schon, 1983, p.viii). Schon sees all practice situations as complex, uncertain, unstable, unique and ridden with value conflicts, and that there is constantly a mismatch between traditional approaches and the real demands of practice (1983, p.18). He says that some practitioners do manage to produce a 'partial synthesis' from the 'babble of voices' in their profession (1983).

Such an understanding of professional practice recognises at its core the multiplicity of contradictions and tensions that defy a linear, problem-solving approach, where there is no conflict over means or ends. Positivist attempts to package, order and control professional knowledge may reduce it to mere techniques that demonstrate greater certainty about the answer than the question, or as Schon says, about problem-solving rather than problem-setting (1983, p.40).

My model played at the edges of this dilemma. While it recognised the tensions in practice, I was perhaps naively confident that I could also provide answers rather than concentrating on the questions. My own contradictions were demonstrated in presumptions about the field welcoming the model as enlightenment, while at the same time I espoused an approach of negotiating knowledge development. In setting the problem, I had named the things to attend to, and I had framed the context in which to attend to them (Schon, 1983). Schon believes this should be a 'bilateral task' (1983, p.231). Unless research is collaborative, this remains a methodological contradiction.

The process and the purpose of political action in the model remain the least resolved in terms of being shared as an appropriate perspective and adopted as feasible practice. I believe this cautious view of political action is also held in the profession generally. It was easier for me as a non-practitioner to rationalise, as I still do, that political action (from vigorous advocacy to confronting abuse of power and privilege) is both legitimate and feasible in and with a rural community, whereas practitioners feel more fully the weight of their workload, and know that political action is time and energy consuming, as well as risky if it does not arise from the will of the constituency, which, in turn, requires sometimes-intensive consciousness raising.

At what point, then, am I, the researcher, overstepping the line of sharer/shaper of knowledge? My values are clearly dominant in this regard. I justify this choice with support from the literature, fully documented in the literature review, but nonetheless it sits in my thesis as testament to my values and ideas, and not those of the field.

Again, I return to the value of a collaborative methodology as the means for negotiating that impasse. Had I sought out practitioners who wished specifically to explore that form of practice with me, we might have resolved the issue of appropriateness (at least for them) as well as examined ways of testing the feasibility of such practice. (As it was, participants agreed that it was congruent with their practice, but that a number of resource barriers stood in the way of their practising in that fashion more fully. Their use of political action was partialised rather than holistic in its identification of issues on which to take action.)

At this stage, without further action research to test the model, I have two versions: a hypothetical and a 'working' one. The former is grounded in the literature, remaining holistic, and prescriptive in part. The latter variation is grounded in practice, where, in keeping with much professional practice, rigorous adherence to a single model is not adopted, and where prior exposure to explicit rural theory-building is largely lacking. This dilemma was insufficiently addressed by my choice of research methodology.

Collaborative research appears to offer methodological and perhaps ideological advantages in pursuing knowledge that is identified by those in the field as significant to them, and in employing a method that mirrors the empowering processes of the practice model. But this assertion contains two further dilemmas. Might it be equally difficult to find practitioners willing and able to devote considerable time to such research, if one of the obstacles to implementing the model was given as lack of time? Second, truly collaborative research may have produced both content and results that were unrecognisable from those that emerged from my work. Would I have been able to relinquish control to that extent? If I had not, collaboration would have been a very unwise path to follow. The direction I took led to a tangible model, amenable to further research. Who knows what would have emerged from a collaborative approach?

The choice of a methodology will be governed by prevailing circumstances. Had I been approached by local practitioners who wished me to work with them on a joint project, a collaborative approach is obvious. Not many situations are as clear-cut. Realistically, the appropriateness of collaboration depends on a range of variables relating to time availability, commitment and practical and theoretical knowledge, as well as assumptions about equality of status, personal meanings of expertise and ownership of knowledge.

CONCLUSION

This chapter has examined the way in which a research journey, made first to accomplish some 'basic mapping of the territory' of rural social work, and subsequently reviewed for reflective purposes, can demonstrate the essential uncertainty and fluidity of research phenomena. The sense of completion I felt at the end of the research is now replaced by a sense of the possibilities that might have arisen from a different methodology. I am aware that unacknowledged assumptions may lead us to believe that our espoused theory does equate with our theory in use when the two may, in fact, be contradictory. I am also aware that the development of a model that proposes to offer a new form of practice is itself an evolving piece of technology that must reflect the time and place within which it will be used. Its implementation will reflect the practitioners' own persona, their values and their experience, because we cannot separate the knower from the known.

REFERENCES

Bailey, R. and Lee, P. (1982) *Theory and Practice in Social Work*, Basil Blackwell, Oxford

Carew, R. (1979) 'The place of knowledge in social work activity', *British Journal of Social Work* vol.9, pp. 349–364

Cook, T.D. and Reichardt, C.S. (1977) *Qualitative and Quantitative Methods in Evaluation Research*, Sage, Beverly Hills

Hardiker, P. and Barker, M. (1981) *Theories of Practice in Social Work*, Academic Press, New York

Lynn, M. (1990) Developing a rural social work practice model, MSW thesis, Monash University, Melbourne

Martinez-Brawley, E.E. (1980) 'Rural social work tenets in the US and Latin America: A cross-cultural comparison', *Community Development Journal*, vol.15, no.3, pp. 167–178

——(1985) 'Rural social work as contextual specialty: Undergraduate focus or graduate concentration?' *Journal of Education for Social Work*, vol. 21, no. 3, pp. 36–42

Pease, B. (1987) 'Doing collaborative and experiential research on theory and practice in social work', *Australian Association of Social Work Education Workshop*, Perth

——(1990) 'Towards collaborative research on socialist theory and practice in social work', in Petruchenia, J. & Thorpe, R. (eds) *Social Change and Social Welfare Practice*, Hale & Iremonger, Sydney, pp. 86–100

Schon, D. A. (1983) *The Reflective Practitioner*, Basic Books, New York

Wharf, B. (1984) 'Towards a leadership role in human services: The case for rural communities', *Second International Institute on Social Work in Rural Areas*, Maine

York, R.O., Denton, R. T. and Moran, J. R. (1989) 'Rural and urban social work practice: Is there a difference?', *Social Casework* April, 1989, pp. 201–209

13   Constructing frameworks from practice: Towards a participatory approach
Ann Ingamells

The study described in this chapter was a qualitative study with 30 Western Australian community workers who are based in a variety of settings at the community, local government and state government levels. The study was undertaken as a postgraduate thesis requirement.

The impetus for the study was my concern that bureaucratic discourse is playing an undue part in the process of defining what community work is and how it should be practised. This discourse is transmitted via funding guidelines, program objectives, organisational expectations, community expectations, 'how to do it' material produced by government departments and, most importantly, the accounting procedures imposed by funding bodies. Under the influence of these kinds of materials it is hardly surprising that workers should begin to talk and think about their work in reductive terms.

It may be expedient for workers to keep quiet about those aspects of their work which are outside funding-body expectations. Their silence, however, means that much of the work is not acknowledged in funding, not legitimised in performance review, poorly resourced in terms of education and training, and not part of a conscious theoretical development process.

Economic-rationalist, bureaucratic discourses tend to be built on an assumption that there is one right way to view the world. Consequently they are inherently ethnocentric, and possibly discriminatory in other ways. At a policy level the economic-rationalist direction is mitigated by a social justice strategy which emphasises rights, equity, access and participation. However, the contradiction of seeking justice for people who are marginalised because they are different within an overarching framework which insists on narrow uniformity is never fully confronted.

As a community worker, I constantly found that a large part of my work involved building relationships with people whose experience of the world was different from my own, and facilitating connections between groups of people whose experience of the world was different from each other's. These relationship processes differ from a general application of interpersonal skills, and yet I found the community practice literature silent about them. When I shifted my own focus to teaching community development I was frustrated by the scant coverage of this in the literature.

This study sought to articulate some of the relationship-building aspects of community practice. I hoped it would provide a beginning discourse that would encourage workers to talk more about the complexities in building relationships at the community level. I also hoped that naming such aspects of the work would bring them greater legitimacy.

REFLECTIONS ON METHOD

At the outset I wanted the study to be as participatory as possible with community workers reflecting on their own experience and engaging collaboratively in the process of constructing meaning. Collaboration, however, is something you cannot force. As Peter Reason says, 'you can't just set up a co-operative inquiry group'. Such a group may come together, but many conditions will affect whether it does and how cooperative it is (Reason, 1988, p.19).

In this instance, it did not come together easily. I was new to Perth, people did not know me; there was a history of attempts to establish community work study and support groups, there was some defensiveness around practice styles and, most importantly, the idea of a group trying to articulate elusive aspects of practice sounded like a time-consuming and perhaps frustrating exercise. I was not getting very far.

I decided then, as I would in any community task, to focus first on building some relationships. I simply set out with a tape recorder and, using a snowballing process, asked a range of workers if they would like to talk with me about their work. I visited them at their workplaces. The process was totally unstructured. The workers themselves decided what to discuss. Sometimes they took me out to meet people and see projects, sometimes we just sat and talked. Always, I explained that I wanted eventually to make the process more collaborative.

Thirty very rich transcripts later, I decided I could not deal with any more material. Workers had been happy to cooperate while I was on their ground, but it was now time to make the shift to shared ground. I was well aware that each of the workers had only their own transcript, whereas I had the overview. Fifteen workers came to the first workshop. Here I fed back a summary of the themes from the transcipts. People had described the kinds of activities, tasks and projects they did, some of the current challenges and tensions they faced. They had told stories of how they came to be where they were, of significant learning experiences along the way, of what they were good at and where they needed to develop, what they liked about their work and which things bothered them. Relationship issues threaded their way through all the stories. At the workshop we discussed this material and the workers told further stories to illustrate their work. From these stories and discussions some common themes arose, which the workers suggested I go away and work with. They wanted to meet again, and were beginning to appreciate the process, but they were clearly designating the hard work of constructing meaning from the diverse data to me.

While I pointed out that a more collaborative approach would produce a more complete picture of practice, the consensus of the group was that it would come together to review anything I wrote, but could not come together for the long hours which would need to be spent on the making-sense process.

Only in retrospect did the momentuous nature of the decision become clear to me. This group of fifteen workers had vested in me the power to construct meaning from their accounts of their practice. The only perspective from which I could authentically do this was my own. Nevertheless, I stayed in touch with workers through the period during which I was working with the material and we did go through all drafts together.

WHOSE REALITY? THE PROCESS OF CONSTRUCTING MEANING

I now had 30 transcripts plus some field notes, and notes from the workshops. These materials represented a very diverse picture of community practice that would lend itself to any number of interpretations. If I chose to codify this material in the usual way of selecting dominant themes, I would undoubtedly reproduce another version of the dominant paradigm of community practice. This was inevitable because we tend to use dominant frameworks to discuss our work. The workers, like me, had learned to think, to interpret their feelings and to construct their practice in ways which are heavily influenced by dominant perspectives, but I knew also, that, like me, they had developed understandings, ideas and practices that were at odds with dominant perspectives. I assumed that these 'other' aspects would offer the way out of hegemonic thinking. Thirty different people sitting down with this data would come out with 30 different pictures of community practice. Within the paradigm of the social construction of reality, this co-existence of multiple realities is acknowledged. Each would have validity and shed some light on practice. My sense of what needed to be identified and acknowledged in practice, based in my own experience of both practice and the literature, and ratified from the workers' accounts of their practice, offered the only starting point. If the workers did not find the emerging picture a useful way of constructing practice, they would need to enter into greater collaboration in order to change the picture.

This recognition that I needed a perspective if I were to make sense of such complex and diverse data overturned my previous assumption that I would follow some process based on grounded theory (Glaser & Strauss, 1967). Grounded theory, I now recognised, would reflect the preponderance of dominant perspectives in the way we talk about our work. It would not necessarily uncover the muted perspectives. An inductive approach would not necessarily challenge the prevailing ideas. On the other hand, I did not have a fully developed theoretical framework for identifying the muted perspectives, so a fully deductive approach was not possible. Feminist research theorists Stanley and Wise suggest that:

> researchers cannot have empty heads in the way that inductivism proposes; nor is it possible that theory is untainted by material experiences in the way that deductivism proposes. (1990, p.22)

To move reflectively between my own experience, the literature and the workers' accounts, while continuously checking the emerging picture with the workers, appeared to combine the best of inductive and deductive approaches.

Once I had authorised myself in this way, the challenge became to work out what my own perspective actually was. I had set out with an interest in the ways in which practice could contribute to making society less sexist, racist and classist, and I had thought a social justice framework within an economic-rationalist paradigm an inadequate approach to this. I thought better practices probably already existed but were rendered invisible by perspectival biases. What I really wanted to know from workers' accounts was what these better practices were. I sensed relationships were an important aspect, but had no theoretical framework for exploring this.

My purpose, then, was, in Patti Lather's words, 'to tell a story that makes a difference not only at the site of thought but also at the site of sociopolitical practice' (Lather, 1991, p.151). The second part of this paper is an abbreviated retelling of this story.

FROM STORIES TO PRACTICE FRAMEWORKS

A female worker who works only with women considered that she had a particularly female way of working. She described a typical start to her working day:

> I pulled into work, and was gathering my things and locking the car. A young woman, a new client, was in the garden. We chatted a bit and picked some flowers. She clearly had something on her mind. She was choosing the flowers carefully. Together we took them inside and found a vase. While she was arranging them, we talked. I was conscious that this was a necessary part of the relationship-building process. This is how it happens. I don't place myself in an expert relationship with the women. If they need counselling it happens simply as part of a conversation. Sometimes we go into the office for privacy, but mostly it happens informally. Other women sometimes join in. In this way they come to talk more to each other and recognise the shared nature of the issues and the social causes of them. Similarly when I have information, say about family law or something, I simply tell them and they tell me how it affects them. We learn things together, rather than my organising things and their participating.
>
> I do consciously ensure that everyone has opportunities to participate at whatever levels they choose, but my work is invisible. When a social task emerges from these informal discussions, the women concerned have an interest and reason for being involved. In this way they make the connection between their personal lives and the policies and social processes around them. I have a male colleague who works in more formal ways. He presents information and counsels more formally, and people look up to him as an expert. His style is caring but not so interactive. People come to think he knows things and they don't. My more interactive style means people listen to themselves and each other as well as to me. I don't stand out as being the expert, but they learn to trust themselves more. The difficulty is that I have trouble describing what it is I actually do. It's hard to write it down on work plans and reports, difficult to gain recognition of my skills from my employer, difficult to acknowledge my own level of skill, even to myself.

This worker sees the world as needing more emphasis on connection. She sees expert and organisational processes which emphasise differences in power and ability as cutting across connection in order to achieve outcomes that enhance the worker's sense of competence.

She went on to describe the limitations in her approach, which largely relate to difficulties in initiating projects when there is no ready response from others, that is when there is a need to cut across connection to get things done:

> I have taken on a very public and political task, the agenda for which came out of a policy forum I participate in. On my good days I think I can do it, but on less optimistic days it looks formidable. On good days I imagine a high level of consensus about the project with people enthusiastically contributing. But the reality is, it will take some force to get this project off the ground. I will have to get people to do things they don't really want to do, or don't have time to do. I'll have to make unilateral decisions to get things moving, and then I wonder is it really worth it.

To be forceful, to risk breaking connection, to express power over others, to assume authoritative status, these all seem to violate some inner code for this worker. She is learning to initiate and is pushing herself in these directions, but she knows that she has to overcome what she supposes is some female conditioning to assume such roles.

I compare this to a male worker who said: 'It's quite clear to me what this community wants, the social profile spells it out.'

Reflecting on why these workers' accounts affected me reveals much about my own experience and perspective. I was a woman, trained by men, reading community practice literature written mainly by men, to do work which was largely with women. The division between the way the field was conceptualised and my experience of it lay along lines of gender. Had I been an Aboriginal person, the ethnocentricity of the frameworks rather than their androcentricity would have been the point of departure. Using myself as the human instrument in this way, I allowed what affected me most in the data to shape the emerging construction. The theory here is that the human being with self-awareness, experience, training and integrity can make very useful assessments of what is going on in complex, indeterminate situations that would be cumbersome, expensive and difficult to make using artificially constructed tools (Lincoln & Guba, 1985, p.192). The checkpoint is the ongoing consultation with the workers, who, at any stage, can indicate that the emerging construction is not a legitimate way of making sense of practice. In working with the data, then, I moved between trusting my own judgment, talking with others and searching the literature. This seems a useful approach to practice research where the researcher is an insider with significant practice experience.

When I moved to the literature I found that Carol Gilligan, writing in the area of feminist psychology and moral development, gave me more insight into the situation described by the worker above than any of the community practice literature:

> In the fall of this year a woman from Memphis sent me a newspaper clipping. Children had been asked to write essays on how to improve their city, and the journalist noticed a difference between essays written by boys and by girls. To the boys, improving the city meant urban renewal as we generally conceive of it: more parks, new buildings, renovations, better streets, more lighting. Girls however wrote about improving the city in a way the reporter found surprising. They suggested strengthening the relationships between people: responding to people in need and taking action to help them. (Gilligan, 1988, p.i)

Gilligan asks why the words 'improving your city' have different meanings for different people, whose meanings will be taken as right or definitive, and what the implications are of speaking in what is considered to be the 'right' language. Could it be that because of our gender conditioning, females and males do have different responses to these kinds of questions and, therefore, do see differently what needs doing at the community level?

Gilligan and her associates at the Harvard Graduate School of Education have evolved an understanding of the way individuals experience themselves and make choices in the world. They have shown that earlier theorists (Piaget (1965) and Kohlberg (1981)) studied mainly masculine psychology, in the light of which women measured up poorly. This masculine psychology posited that at a certain stage in development the individual experiences himself as an autonomous, rational, choosing agent, and that healthy moral choices are then made in the light of principles such as justice, fairness, and equality. Gilligan calls this the justice perspective.

Through study after study of women and girls, Gilligan and associates posit that women often experience themselves as connected to, rather than separated from, others. This means that they may resist the detachment associated with the model of the autonomous rational chooser, and instead pursue a line of thinking which considers people in their context. They may consider, for example, what will happen to the relationships in terms of any choices which are made. Bardige, from her study of adolescent girls, posited that girls who appear to exemplify lower levels of cognitive functioning in early adolescence may in fact be resisting the detachment which characterises abstract or formal reasoning (Bardige, 1988, p.101).

Gilligan says that:

> By the age of eleven, most children can solve moral problems both in terms of rights (a justice model) and in terms of response (a care approach). The fact that a person adopts one approach in solving a

problem does not mean that he or she does not know or appreciate others. (Gilligan, 1988, p.iii)

However, the studies do show that the approach taken by men and boys tends to be the justice approach and the approach taken by women and girls tends to be the care approach. Formal education makes girls more aware of the justice approach as the socially approved model, so that on entering public-world positions, this is likely to be the approach women will adopt. Clearly, most of the frameworks for public-world policy and action come from this masculine tendency to value the justice perspective.

Gilligan affirmed my own sense that where I stand, as a woman trying to do community work in a gendered society, affects what I see as needing doing. Her writing, especially in the light of the worker's story above, lifted the veil which obscured the idea that the view women have from their own standpoint as women has public and social relevance. While they may not want to limit themselves to it, neither should they necessarily deny it, or trade it for some more prestigious viewpoint.

Although women may incorporate the views and experiences of more masculine, instrumental perspectives into their frameworks in order to work more holistically, they do not need to deny those more expressive, interactive, context-specific aspects of their experience. In fact, in valuing the instrumental aspects of the work over the expressive (even by talking about them more), and by letting the expressive aspects remain invisible, we contribute to a sexist definition of the field. On the other hand, if all resources pertain to the instrumental aspects of the work, women alone will not want to carry the invisible burden.

A contemporary gender-aware community practice would need to be one in which women and men developed capacities to work across the whole range of tasks, expressive and instrumental, which had previously been divided along gender lines. In some ways this is easier for women, because the instrumental side of the equation has been spelled out quite clearly along the way, so there is a body of information on it, whereas little has been written about the interactive/connecting tasks, which women have tended to do invisibly. Further, there is an incentive for women to learn the instrumental tasks, which make the worker feel more powerful and bring credibility, status and resources. There is little incentive for men to learn the expressive tasks because they make the worker feel less powerful, carry no status or resources, and often bring little acknowledgment.

Gilligan's work has special relevance to community practice because it highlights the contradictions in trying to build community using a justice rather than a connecting/interactive perspective. The justice perspective is more appropriate to the individual/society framework (which sees society as autonomous individuals linked by contracts, obligations and roles) than to a community framework, which sees people as connected and inextricably affecting each other by their choices and actions. The connection framework implies responsibility to actual people in concrete situations, whereas the justice perspective implies responsibility to generalised ideas and abstract principles.

Community practice is perhaps one field where the two perspectives, with their two frameworks, are both needed. The challenge is to have both frameworks equally developed and to be clear which is most appropriate when, rather than to have one in an obviously dominant position with its language and concepts constantly co-opting those of the other.

At this point in the picture-making process I paused to reflect on the wider implications of the emerging frame. Was I constructing a framework that would encourage women to continue taking responsibility for work for which they were traditionally devalued? No. I hope I was asserting the need for both men and women to do this necessary work. Was I constructing an ideal community model along the lines of Tonnies' *Gemeinschaft* (1957)? Feminists would critique any such suggestion because of the patriarchal and oppressive connotations of the traditional small community. Iris Marion Young (1990), for example, critiques the ideal of small face-to-face community at several levels. However, I do not propose face-to-face community but rather the recognition that people, across the globe, are connected and affect each other. I saw this emerging framework, then, not as suggesting a return to consensus politics, but rather as contributing to a politics of difference in the face of a worldwide imposition of the world view of economic rationalism.

Anna Yeatman, in her attempts to establish a politics of difference, says we need to let go of the individuality/separateness/mastery association and develop:

> An individuality which understands itself in a relational way, that is to say, understands the interactional bases of a self concept and the kind of interactional culture necessary to foster and support the participation of all. (Yeatman, 1990, p.290)

She claims that, paradoxically, within such an interactional framework the particular person will have more voice and receive greater acknowledgment than has been the case under a philosophy of individualism. This is because the creation of spaces for interaction and the development of voice and of skills which allow for negotiation of meaning across difference is valued over any unitary direction or imposition of order.

This research process of moving between workers' stories and the literature in order to construct a theoretical framework took on special relevance when it became clear how rarely the momentum of academic theorising and the momentum of practice actually intersect. I think we were all enlivened by the new insights into practice the theory offered.

To return to workers' stories, then, it is not only female workers who struggle to acknowledge connection. The men who participated in this study also recognise the anti-community role of hegemonic masculinity. One worker explained how he had tried to bring about a festival using a developmental, community-building approach. The idea was to foster the creativity already existing in the local community and to encourage people to develop their own input to the festival in terms of a range of music, art, craft, drama and other activities, and to let the shape of the festival emerge from a mix of planned and spontaneous activities along these lines. In this way the people who came to the festival would be participants rather than consumers. While the idea was initially accepted, a struggle then ensued within and between all players, the funding body, the organising committee, and members of the community. Preconceived notions of how festivals should be organised were at odds with a new and little-known way of doing things. This worker struggled for the language to embrace the vision. He described a commercial-style street parade:

> . . . row after row of plastic humans, sitting immobile astride tarted-up utilities, sporting toothy, frozen smiles, with disembodied hands waving mechanically à la Elizabeth R.

Dolled-up people on floats acting a role prescribed by their commercial sponsor with consumers passively looking on suggests people alienated from themselves as well as from each other. Describing a more inspiring scene, he goes on:

> . . . around the corner came an alive, dancing cavorting tribe of shimmering dancing bodies with some funky beat going down . . . an alive snakin' mess of people, funco-pating from one place to another, picking up another tribe of funksters to sway and samba together to create an alive jumping streetscape of people having fun.
> (Genat, 1992)

With festivals, as with all community activity, if the emphasis is placed too heavily on organisation the result is domestication rather than liberation. Domestication means that people trim their input to fit with the organiser's vision. A more developmental approach begins with the people. The worker facilitates rather than organises; the vision grows as various people contribute their own creative effort to the process.

If the emphasis is too heavily placed on development, there will be no denouement, no event and no sense of achievement. Both development and organisation are necessary. The two exist in tension, but because, as a society, we have tended to place all the emphasis and all the resources on the organisational aspect, we have robbed the process of its developmental and community-building potential. To the extent that we do this we foster domestication, dependence, alienation and perhaps cynicism.

Each one of us, whether on a committee, in the community, or within the funding body, has experienced the overwhelming cultural emphasis on organisational processes at the expense of developmental processes, so the struggle happens within as well as between people and groups.

The framework we are trying to develop, then, is a framework that emphasises connection and the interactive processes which facilitate it. Two important dimensions of this framework are the expressive/instrumental and the developmental/organisational axes. The expressive and the developmental processes are the underdeveloped arms which need emphasising and enacting.

Another dimension of the framework is base/survival. Worker's stories continually raised the difficulties of doing community work without a sound base. Base usually means organisation or locality, but in this study it came to mean more. Survival can mean survival in the job, survival as a community worker (community work positions are often converted to less challenging welfare-delivery positions), survival politically, and survival in terms of health. Base is not something external and objective to the worker, rather it is constituted of many external and internal threads, all of which vary in their stability over time. In the study we worked with six strands of base, three external to the worker and three internal. The external were the political economy, the organisational context and the locality. The internal were the worker's self/social awareness, the personal supports and the practice framework. Base is centrally about connection. Unless the worker has strong connections somewhere, survival will be at stake. Some workers had no organisational supports and uncertain funding, but a strong internal sense of mission and some good friends. Others worked in non-supportive organisations but in a locality which had strong community networks and supports. Still others worked in politically and economically troubled localities but had excellent practice frameworks for coping with this.

One interesting aspect of base is the worker's own self/social

awareness. This is something deeper than the usual left/right ideological axes traditionally used to characterise workers. Some workers
with a sound structural analysis incorporate this into their work via
enhanced awareness of the ways in which the expectations of funding
bodies and organisations, and the workers' own cultural, gender and
class expectations, affect the people they work with. Challenging
these expectations is part of the developmental process. Such workers
are prepared to begin dismantling their own conditioned assumptions
and expectations. Without such a high level of self-awareness, sometimes the very analysis which sustains our social justice framework
can separate us from the people we want to work with.

A worker discussed the difficulty she had in establishing relationships with women in her community. These were women from a
cultural background steeped in patriarchy. Her own cultural background was the same, but she had been educated in Australia and
had gained a strong feminist perspective. She said: 'At first I thought
that if I only did what they wanted to do, I would do nothing, for
they only wanted to stay at home.'

She organised activity after activity, but they failed to turn up,
regardless of how much interest they seemed to show when she
consulted them. In order to really reach them on their own ground
she had to reach back across her own Australian socialisation to her
origins in that same culture. Her initial impatience had more to do
with the effort this required of her, and the threat it posed to her
own current identity, than with anything the women did. She needed
to bridge the gap between her need to see herself as competent and
the need to put herself in their position. Her abstract analysis of the
situation existed only in her own head, but the women were based
in the complex matters of their own lives, where every move would
affect something and someone else, and would risk unbalancing an
already precarious status quo.

Theirs was the only possible starting point. Reflection allowed
this worker to see that from her own perspective, with her clear
analysis of the situation, she could see their options and feel impati-
ent with their lack of action; once she crossed to their perspective
and took on board all the aspects of their lives they were trying to
hold together, she felt as immobilised as they did. From this starting
point the steps that could be taken were smaller, but she found she
did have the skills and trust in process to begin some good work
with the women. With a secure organisational base and several other
more conventional projects in place, together with a relatively strong
practice framework, this worker could take risks which made her
internal sense of self temporarily shaky for the sake of connection
to others. With other aspects of base in place a risk of this kind is
a calculated risk, without them it would be foolhardy.

Another dimension is the feelings/rationality one. A myth exists in some Anglo cultures that public-world processes are built on rationality. Feeling is obscured and denied. Many stories illustrated this dimension. Several workers were involved with housing issues. A worker involved with a group of people who had been evicted from relatively cheap housing because of urban development saw both the strengths and weaknesses of relying on a discourse of tenants' rights to make this public. This discourse does translate the personal meanings of a marginalised group into the public world and demand the attention of the decision makers. It also, however, shields people from each other. The people who move into the gentrified houses never have to face the feelings of the people they have displaced. The planners and developers never have to confront the personal needs (ambition, need for ascendancy, need to be seen as competent, desire to impose their conceptions of order, fear of failure) which have driven them to promote such developments. All of the negative consequences and diffficult feelings are displaced onto the least powerful group of people involved. These people might then come to see themselves as victims and rely unduly on trying to force governments to respond to their needs.

A worker described how he had worked with a community affected by a government planning proposal. There was a great deal of anger in the community. The planners' logic and the community feeling seemed poles apart. Using theatrical techniques in a public meeting, the community members made graphic presentations of what the proposed plan would mean to their lives. In other words, they drew the planners into their own life worlds rather than meet the planners at the level of abstract discourse.

The implication here is that power is located not only in institutions and particular people but also in discourses. In the connected framework, people work developmentally to reflect on their own realities, conduct dialogue with each other, and generate discourses which give public-world expression to their perspective, thereby contesting the co-optive influences of dominant discourses.

This poses a central tension between developmental work in the community and the organisational assumptions of bureaucracies which fund community practice. If an underlying assumption of public world process is that rationality will predominate and feelings will be 'managed' into the background, relegated to private life, or pushed out to marginalised groups, how will community workers respond? Will they become managers of feelings and tensions in the community on behalf of the bureaucracies which fund them or will they reverse the pendulum and re-weave feelings back into public life—thereby challenging major assumptions, values and discourses?

This dimension points to a possible relationship between devalued and marginalised groups of people and devalued aspects of ourselves. A linking element in the workers' stories on which I have focused is that the workers saw themselves as part of the developmental process, needing to reclaim denied parts of themselves in order to make the necessary connections.

FOREVER FRAMING

These are familiar stories. When we bring them together and focus on their meaning another picture of practice emerges. This particular picture takes the connections between people, rather than autonomous individuals, as the central assumption about the social world.

This framework acknowledges, and offers ways of working with, the complexity of a social world in which all people and all social understandings and events are in a continuous process of interaction, shaping, and being shaped by, each other. This is why the process of framing is developmental, for the goals change as we change and as our understandings change.

Without frameworks, many faces of the multifaceted activity of community building are impossible to articulate. Workers have contributed more to the development of this framework than I have been able to convey in this chapter. Framework building is, however, a time-consuming and uncertain task. In the pressured contexts of day-to-day work environments there are few incentives to do it. But the work of framing is itself a necessary part of practice. Further, this is not an alternative frame, but an additional one, which means that the skilled worker works with intersecting and sometimes contradictory frames, that is justice and connected frames together, along with many possible others. In this way practice approaches the multidimensionality of the social life it responds to.

In many ways social processes have moved more to the right since this study began, and the environment is even less conducive now to building a discourse which emphasises connection, interaction and reflection. However, the processes of the study have clarified for me that naming obscured parts of our experience not only generates new possibilities for action, it also opens up new internal territory and allows new possibilities for thoughts and feelings. Community building is part of the struggle not to be caged by limiting frameworks like economic rationalism, but to continuously seek ways of keeping the whole range of human energies engaged in the processes of living.

I had hoped that this study would involve a number of workers in reflection and dialogue about their work. The espoused theory was that through the rigorous processes of reflecting and constructing meaning, workers would participate in creating new discourses about their work. In fact, the participation of the workers was intermittent and the discourse produced reflects my own perspective rather than a genuinely shared picture. Moreover, the enhanced understanding of community practice which comes from deep immersion in the topic was mine rather than being fully shared. Patti Lather says: 'Social relations mediate the construction of knowledge; who speaks for who becomes a central question' (Lather,1991, p.91).

Although this study was about working across difference in the community, the workers who stayed with the study were, for the most part, those who shared similar perspectives. Those workers who had very different experiences and perspectives pulled out or became silent. Nor do I think the oppositional elements present in those who stayed with the study were made explicit within the group. We did not manage to create an interactive space in which all the different voices of the 30 workers could be heard, but we did raise the issue of difference, the workers did provide checks on my own theorising, some of them were encouraged to theorise about their own practice more, and we did pave the way for a more collaborative venture in the future. We did not reach full collaboration, but there were genuine moments of collaboration. As Peter Reason says: 'The co-operative inquiry can range from full collaboration through all stages of inquiry—to genuine dialogue and consultation at key moments' (Reason, 1988, p.9).

I am more than ever inclined to believe that the best practice is a reflective practice. We have separated practice and research for too long. Now, getting them to closely relate to each other is quite a challenge. Colin Peile, who also calls for a much closer linking of practice and research, offers a hopeful note to end on:

> The universal unity of practice/research means that everyone must be considered a practitioner researcher. This recognises that everyone is at once both making sense of and trying to create the world they live in. (Peile,1988, p.79)

NOTE

Acknowledgments are due to the 30 workers whose reflections on their work made the study possible, and also to Fran Crawford and Anne Wearne, who guided me through a complex research process. The limitations of this chapter are mine, not theirs.

REFERENCES

Bardige, B. (1988) 'Things so finely human: Moral sensibilities at risk in adolescence' in Gilligan, C., Victoria Ward, J., *et al.*, (eds) *Mapping the Moral Domain*, Harvard University Press, Cambridge, pp.87–110

Genat, B. (1992) Setting up and running a community development project, unpublished paper, Perth

Gilligan, C. (1988). Preface in Gilligan *et al.*, *Mapping the Moral Domain*, Harvard University Press, Cambridge

Glaser, B. and Strauss, A., (1967) *The Discovery of Grounded Theory*, Aldine, Chicago

Kohlberg, L. (1981) *The Philosophy of Moral Development: Moral Stages and the Idea of Justice*, Harper & Row, San Francisco

Lather, P. (1991) *Getting Smart*, Routledge, New York

Lincoln, Y. and Guba, E.G. (1985) *Naturalistic Inquiry*, Sage, Beverly Hills

Peile, C. (1988) 'The unity of research and practice: Creative practitioner research for social workers', in E. Ryan (ed.) *Change and Continuity in Australian Social Work*, Longman Cheshire, Melbourne, pp.69–83

Piaget, J. (1965) *The Moral Judgment of the Child*, Free Press, New York

Reason, P. (ed.) (1988) *Human Inquiry in Action*, Sage, London

Stanley, L. and Wise, S. (1990) 'Method, methodology and epistemology', in L. Stanley (ed.) *Feminist Praxis*, Routledge, London, pp.20–60

Tonnies, F. (1957) *Community and Society*, Harper & Row, New York

Yeatman, A. (1990) 'A feminist theory of social differentiation', in Nicholson, L.J. (ed.) *Feminism/Postmodernism*, Routledge, New York, pp.281–298

Young, I.M. (1990) 'The ideal of community and the politics of difference', in Nicholson, L.J. (ed.) *Feminism/Postmodernism*, Routledge, New York, pp.300–323

Part V

Making practice research public

14 Empowering practitioners to publish: A writer's and a publisher's perspectives

Elizabeth Rabbitts and Jan Fook

We all know that writing up and publishing the results of one's work are supposed to be the culmination of research. Yet how much work remains in draft form in the heads and filing cabinets of countless social workers? There are the standard excuses: 'not enough time'; 'it's easier said than done'; 'most of what is published is not useful to practitioners anyway'. These may all be true, but are not really excuses. We don't have much time, but why have we prioritised other activities over writing? Writing for publication can be excruciatingly difficult, but which social worker has not had to engage in painful activity? And if most of what is published is not useful to practitioners, isn't it up to us to begin to change that? Once the excuses have run out, we are still confronted with the fact that if we want our work to have broad influence, we really need to have it published in some form. Of course there are other useful ways in which we can publicise our work, through speaking at conferences or running workshops, for example, but there are many audiences that can only be reached by the published word.

The question then becomes how to minimise the time and pain of publishing in order to ensure that work which is relevant to practitioners is more widely accessible. This chapter is about examining some of the preconceived notions of writing and publishing that often make it difficult for us to sit down to the task and, once we've sat down, dog our every step so that we make overly difficult work of it. The first part of this chapter will examine these assumptions from the perspective of a writer (Jan Fook) and reformulate some guiding principles drawn from the experience of publishing.

The second part will be written from the perspective of a journal editor (Elizabeth Rabbitts), commenting on the first part and drawing out further principles from editorial experience.

PUBLISHING FROM A WRITER'S PERSPECTIVE

Initial assumptions about publishing

On reflection, I find that early in my writing career I held a number of assumptions which made writing and submitting for publication seem quite daunting, and the prospect of rejection seem so traumatic that I could have easily been discouraged for life.

First, I assumed that the processes of writing and publishing were the same thing—that being able to prepare well-written material was tantamount to getting my work published. This meant that I agonised over draft after draft until it did indeed feel as if drops of blood were being squeezed from my forehead, as Elspeth Browne so graphically describes (1990, p.1)

Second, I assumed that whatever I published had to be 'academic'. This meant, to me, that it had to be intensely theoretical, could not be descriptive, must contain numerous references (the more the better), could not be personal in style, and must be full of ideas (the more the better). Moreover, it must be original, preferably also the last word on the subject, and hopefully so earth-shattering that it would stop everyone dead in their tracks. (I, like most of us, feared being ridiculed for not saying anything new, or worse, saying something everyone already knew.)

Third, it followed logically (I thought) that any work which met these criteria would immediately be accepted for publication. By implication, then, any work that was rejected was obviously not original, earth-shattering or important. In short, a piece of writing's acceptance or rejection was the ultimate comment on the worth of my ideas.

Naturally, my fourth assumption was that reviewers of material were necessarily fair and objective, professional arbiters of what is important in the knowledge and discourse of the profession.

My experiences with publishing and writing

I recall, with a little amusement and a lot of pain, my first journal rejection. Despite my preparation for the disappointment, and the pointed kindness of the reviewers, I remember driving off to a community meeting in tears. I still wear the watch given to me by my partner as consolation. Many rejections later, after maulings by less kind reviewers, and after my writing was labelled 'turgid' at least twice (I am convinced this is one of the favourite terms of reviewers), I was forced to examine some of those early assumptions.

Why was it that some people reacted really well to my papers yet when I submitted them to journals they were rejected outright? Why did some reviewers recommend that I submit to other journals if they did not consider the material good enough for their own? How was it that some reviewers could become fixated on grammar (for example, split infinitives) and ignore the ideas in a paper? How could I account for the fact that papers I thought were mediocre were received enthusiastically while others which for me were ground-breaking were dismissed as banal?

My re-formulated theory of the practice of publishing

Since my experience taught me that the same paper could be loved by one audience and loathed by another, I was forced to arrive at that most simple of adages, that *publishing is about communicating effectively* and is therefore about *writing in the appropriate way for the appropriate audience.* In short, I came to recognise something my social work training should have told me all along, that *publishing is simply about writing which is appropriate to the context.* So good writing in one context does not necessarily make for publishable material. Whether material is publishable or not depends on the forum and audience to which it is directed, and whether the ideas in it are communicated in terms that are meaningful and valued in this context. Publishing is a *social* process and needs to be recognised as such if we are to engage in it successfully. It is therefore important to recognise that there are myriad different publishing forums, each involving a particular audience, and therefore we need to market material in the way in which it will be best understood and appreciated by that audience.

Strictly speaking, it is difficult to define what is a publication and what is not. By convention, the term 'publication' usually refers to printed material which is widely circulated and available to the public, and in this sense material which is accepted for publication by a commercial or professional publisher is usually rated most highly. People sometimes regard 'in-house' publications (those printed for circulation within one's own organisation) less highly, presumably because they are less widely distributed and have presumably not been subjected to outside anonymous review. They may, however, be most appropriate, depending on the intended audience. The issue of what is a publication and what is not is hotly debated and, like most things, highly political. (In this chapter I am speaking mostly about publishing in outlets which subject all submissions to anonymous peer review, since these forums are generally regarded as the most exacting.) The main question, however, is which forum is most appropriate for the ideas you wish to disseminate.

In this sense, getting material published depends not on the inherent worth of your ideas but on your ability to gauge accurately the culture of the forum to which you wish to submit the material, the audience to which you wish to speak, and the style and format which will best communicate your message. In the next section I will offer some pointers to assist you in making these decisions.

In this sense, also, the acceptance or rejection of material is not a comment on the inherent worth of the ideas, but only on whether you've gauged the forum accurately. As a colleague of mine is fond of saying, there is no such thing as a bad (unpublishable) idea, only an inappropriately expressed or submitted idea.

This is a potentially empowering point, I believe, because in reaffirming the *contextual* nature of our work it shifts the focus from any essential judgment of it to the ways in which we construct and communicate about it in different situations. In other words, it firmly locates with us the ability to construct our work in the way we choose to suit the forum of our choice.

This leads neatly to my next point, which is that if publishing is mostly about directing appropriate ideas in the most effective way to the audience in question, then it is immaterial whether or not the ideas are 'the last word', or 'world-shattering' or 'academic'. What is important is that they are communicated so that they can be understood in meaningful (and hopefully useful) ways. Arguably, the simplest and most banal idea, if expressed in such a way that the audience engages with it and finds it reaffirming or challenging, can be important. Some of the simplest ideas, and simplest articles, can have the most impact on you. It may be that much of the food for your own research and publication lies in simply expressing your ideas in a way you think will be meaningful and helpful to other people. And given the multiplicity of social work practice settings, surely there is room for a multiplicity of ways of expressing our ideas.

Lastly, my experience emphasises something else I should have known all along, which is that there is a *politics* to publishing, as to everything else. French (1993) gives an excellent overview of the politics involved in all aspects of the publishing process—in decisions about what to say, where to say it, and the ethics involved. To feel confident about publishing, it is important to bear in mind that reviewers are ordinary people, and therefore their taste, opinions and levels of competence differ, just as do writers'. There are good and bad reviewers, reviewers with whom you will disagree, reviewers whom you respect, and reviewers who have the power to damn your work forever. Accept that this is the case, and treat their work critically. Successful publishing is, on one level, about using your reviewers' feedback critically. Don't accept their every word as the breath of God and a final judgment on the worth of your ideas, but at the same time do glean from it that which you think important, relevant or helpful in improving your work, and in deciding where you should perhaps submit that article. And remember, reviewers' comments tell you as much about them as they do about your work. Learn what reviewers do and don't like, and learn to write in ways which impress them (favourably).

Some 'handy hints' and practical guidelines

I do not wish to give the impression that successful publishing is *only* about a change of attitude and assumptions and an uncovering of the politics involved. Some fairly clear practice guidelines are indicated by this process, and I will outline them as they have been useful to me in my publishing endeavours. For an alternative discussion see Sheafor *et al.* (1988, pp.161–165).

There are really four main questions (and a few sub-questions) to ask yourself when you decide you want to publish something:

1   What do I want to say? How complex is it really? (TOPIC)
2   Why do I want to say it? Why do I think it is important and what outcome would I like? (REASON and PURPOSE)
3   To whom do I want to say it? (FORUM and AUDIENCE)
4   How do I want to say it? What status am I claiming? (STYLE and ORGANISATION)

Topic
When you identify your topic, it is important that you be able to express it as *one* main idea (in one line). The more simply you can express it the better. Your topic might be an argument (for example, 'social workers need to do more practice research'); a description (for example, 'a report on a study of social workers' involvement in practice research'); an illustrative piece (for example, 'social workers' difficulties with practice research'); or a mixture, of course. C. Wright Mills, that most accomplished of authors, offers a handy hint here—it may be helpful to distinguish the *prose* from the *pose* (1970, p.240). In other words, try to differentiate between what you want to say and the way you think you might be expected to say it in learned circles. Mills suggests that you ask yourself how difficult or complex your subject is after all. Do you really need jargon and wordy ways of expressing it? Later you can assume the appropriate pose—first you need to clarify for yourself what it is you want to say.

Reason and purpose
You should be able to articulate why you think your topic is important and what you hope will come out of it, since you will have to state these things in your writing and again when you 'sell' the writing to editors, reviewers and readers. The more simply you can do so the better. Some useful questions are: What motivated you to write about this? How did you come to be interested? What will happen if we don't know about it? Will it change our thinking or practices in any way? Why should people other than yourself be interested? What do you hope readers will do, or how do you hope they will be affected as a result of reading your publication?

Audience and forum
Who do you most wish to influence with your publication and how will they best be reached? This involves questions of the type of readership (narrow professional, academic, broad disciplinary, members of lay public, consumer groups) and circulation (numbers of copies, areas and processes of distribution, breadth of advertising, cost of publication). It is generally agreed that journal articles (particularly refereed ones) have a narrower circulation than books, but on the other hand, you may wish to target a specific group of people who you know normally reads a particular journal. Most journals contain notes about their readership and circulation. A handy reference is Mendelsohn (1992), which is a guide to social work journals, and most disciplines have an equivalent reference work listing journals, publication philosophies and publication requirements. The best way to gauge the 'culture' of a journal is to flip through a few issues, taking note of the types of articles therein. Only send your paper to a journal if you think it fits the publication's general style and type.

The same rules apply when selecting a publisher for a book. Select publishers with a track record of publishing social work books, or which you know have published work similar to your proposed work.

The different forums in which you can publish vary enormously. The politics of publishing with commercial and non-commercial publishers may differ, as it may with self-published work. Journals may be refereed, non-refereed (e.g. newsletters or bulletins), local, international, academic or professional. Other types of publications include pamphlets, reports, monographs, book reviews, letters, comments, conference papers, and working papers. Generally speaking, commercial, refereed and international work is the more difficult to publish, often because criteria are narrower, or the work has to demonstrate 'sellability'. If you are not used to publishing, it is probably wise to start with the less difficult forums. For example, a working paper circulated among colleagues can in time turn into a conference paper and, later, a journal article. The task can also seem less daunting if you tackle it with a group of colleagues, but of course your own personal work style is the important arbiter here. (In Chapter 10, Martin Ryan discusses some of the pros and cons of collaborative work.)

Style and organisation
Your chosen forum and audience will in part influence the style, format and organisation of your paper. Journals normally stipulate the approximate length of articles, and in some cases the style and content. Negotiations with book publishers will also include discussion of style, content and organisation. If in doubt about whether your material is appropriate, discuss your concerns with the publisher or editor. This can not only save you from wasting a lot of time but also help set up a fruitful working relationship.

Mills suggests asking 'What status am I claiming?' (1970, p.240) in writing your work. In other words, what position do you wish to assume in relation to your readers, and what is the best position to assume in order to communicate your message most effectively? Do you wish to be seen as an authoritative expert, dispassionate researcher, engaged clinician, or sympathetic colleague? Do you wish to dazzle readers with your wit and intelligence, persuade them to your viewpoint, establish the credibility of your findings, or move them with your experience? As I have indicated earlier, the formal academic style is only one form of publication. This might be most appropriate if you wish to gain acceptance for your work in academic circles, but may be counterproductive if you wish readers to examine their own experience.

One of the biggest writing hurdles I have had to overcome (and I may not have done so entirely) was the assumption that I had to cram every bit of knowledge I had into every sentence in order to demonstrate my mastery of the material. I suspect that writing my thesis engendered bad writing habits that have carried over into every other forum. I found it most liberating to realise that I was probably writing in this turgid way because of my own needs—I was avoiding expressing myself in clear and simple terms for fear that I would be labelled simple and my work ridiculed. I have in fact found it far more challenging to write clearly, because it means my own thinking needs to be clear. I have formed the habit now of questioning the need for long sentences, a string of adjectives or qualifiers, or more than one idea in one sentence. Just who am I trying to impress?

In the following section, Elizabeth Rabbitts talks about the use of the first person ('I'/'we') and suggests that in inexperienced writers this can imply a tendency towards self-promotion. It is always useful to bear in mind, I think, how our language might be interpreted by others despite our intentions. However, from the perspective of a writer, I have found the use of the first person enabling. Much of my early writing was painstakingly 'third person' and passive, in line with traditional academic requirements. When I wrote about theory, this made the ideas seem even more distant from me, and I often found myself doing mental gymnastics to reframe my ideas in the passive voice, which seemed to make their expression even less clear. When I discovered that many academic forums now accept the first person, my writing became much clearer, and there was less 'abstractified' distance between the ideas as I first conceived them and as I expressed them on paper. I suspect that the decision about what person and voice you use will be determined chiefly by what you are comfortable with and by the tone you would like to communicate to your readers. There are also, as Elizabeth's and my accounts bear out, different views about the desirability of the use of the first person, so it may be helpful to seek advice about how your writing comes across to someone else.

For me, questions of style (academic or personal, use of first or third person, passive or active voice), and organisational questions (about number of references, use of sub-headings, and so on) become secondary to these broader questions of audience, forum and purpose. Elizabeth Rabbitts includes in her section following a very helpful list of the types of questions that reviewers ask in order to assess the publishability of the work. Save yourself some trauma and ask yourself the questions first.

Whichever forum and audience you decide upon, it is important to bear in mind that there are still a few conventions which, if followed, should make your work more publishable (unless it is a purely literary piece). There should be a recognisable introduction (which states clearly the topic and aim of your paper/book and justifies its significance), body (containing the main arguments, content), and conclusion (which summarises your paper/book and indicates further directions). If you are writing up the results of an empirical study, there are clear conventions for its organisation (introduction, literature review, results, discussion, conclusion). If in doubt, look at a few examples and copy the layout.

Schilling *et al.* (1985) make a worthwhile point about constructing papers that address an audience made up primarily of practitioners. They argue that conventional formats for research papers often do not meet the needs and interests of practitioners. They also make some excellent suggestions for targeting papers to practising social workers, such as the use of examples, developing clear implications of the research for practice, and writing in a tone sympathetic to practitioners.

Once you have thought through these four main questions (topic, reason/purpose, forum/audience, style/organisation), you should have enough material to write the abstract or proposal of your book or paper. Another useful reference that contains practical guidelines around these basic decisions is Williams and Hopps (1987). As well, commercial publishers may prescribe a book proposal format that addresses the issues they regard as important. Below, Elizabeth Rabbitts discusses some of the ins and outs of marketing, which is a particular issue in commercial publishing and can be crucial to getting a book contract.

Now that we have covered those aspects of writing that are the author's responsibility and you are well on your way to clarifying what, how and where you want to publish, you need to be aware of the intricacies of the publication process from the other side.

THE PUBLISHER'S PERSPECTIVE

Jan Fook is right. Writing for publication can be 'excruciatingly difficult'. On the other hand, it has the potential to be a most satisfying and rewarding experience. How do you optimise your chances of achieving this outcome? The trick, perhaps, is to treat the process as a challenge to be faced rather than a problem to be endured.

As editor of *Australian Social Work*, and as an author, I have come to view the publication process as a little like the production of a play, in which there are many challenges to be faced and overcome.

In a play, the first idea of the playwright evolves into a script. However, the script at first rehearsal is not necessarily the script that is performed on opening night. The script is considered by a professional audience (the director, the actors) and modified in the light of their knowledge and experience of what will most effectively communicate the author's ideas.

Similarly, in publishing, an author's first idea progresses to a written communication which is submitted to a publisher. The draft is not necessarily the text that appears in the published edition. The draft is considered by a professional audience (for example, the reviewers, editor), who suggest modifications in the light of their knowledge and experience of what will most effectively communicate the author's ideas to the readership of the publication.

For me, the challenges involved in this evolution from idea to publication fall into two groups: the *challenges in writing for publication* and the *challenges in dealing with publishers*. An exploration of these challenges follows.

Challenges in writing for publication

Most authors are beset with doubts when deciding whether or not to write for publication. Three recurring concerns stand out: the need to be convinced that the project is publishable, the fear of rejection, and concerns about the effort involved in writing for publication. Dealing with these doubts is essential to successful publishing.

Convincing yourself that your ideas are publishable
There are three aspects to convincing yourself that your ideas are publishable. First, it is essential to examine *what are the ideas and information* you want to share and *why* you think it is important to share them with others. If you do not believe in the value of your writing, it is hard to write with conviction and hence to convince others of your work's value.

Second, it is important to consult with others to find out if anyone else agrees that your ideas may be publishable. However, in my experience, it is more helpful to consult knowledgeable colleagues you trust rather than friends (Rabbitts, 1990). Friends are rarely impartial and may give you false hope. In addition, they are not necessarily representative of the audience you are writing for. There is no need to go as far as Pope suggests—'Get your enemies to read your works in order to mend them for your friend is so much your second self that he will judge too like you' (1709)—but the opinion of impartial trusted colleagues may be a better barometer of success in the publishing arena than the opinion of friends.

A third step in the decision-making process is to take the time to find out what else has been written around the topic and to consult with a research expert in the planning and reporting of any research project. A difficult task for all editors is telling authors that they have duplicated someone else's research, or that the methodology they have used is flawed. Unfortunately, no amount of rearrangement of statistics will produce meaningful results from inappropriately collected data.

So, having examined what you want to share and decided that it may be publishable, you face another challenge—the fear of rejection.

Overcoming the fear of rejection
In pursuing publication, you expose yourself and your work to the publishing industry and here the potential for rejection always exists. To confront and overcome this fear is an enormous hurdle for

authors. I have found it useful to face this challenge at the outset. To examine the reasons for your fears and then deal with them can be a liberating experience that enhances your writing. The anxiety that accompanies the fear of rejection inhibits creativity and this includes the ability to write freely and to organise ideas. The writing that results is less appealing to a publisher.

Once a piece of work is accepted for publication, you expose your work to general public scrutiny and the possibility of rejection on a different level. Rejection may now come in the form of negative printed reviews of your book or article, of poor sales figures or of disparaging comments, either verbal or written.

Anyone who ventures into the publication arena must be prepared to face the worst scenario and then decide whether or not to accept the challenge. Not all authors end up publishing in their chosen forum. Some have to accept alternative outlets for their work. Perhaps, instead of a book or article, they might present the work at a conference, seminar or staff meeting. Even well-established authors sometimes have their work rejected.

Making the effort required to have the piece of writing published
Any author may shelve a writing project before writing a word if daunted by the effort involved in becoming a published author.

It is not enough simply to write what you want to write the way you want to write it. You must meet the requirements of a publisher, as Jan Fook discovered, even if these requirements are not necessarily related to the worth of the piece of writing.

All publishers have certain basic requirements that throw out challenges to the author. These include:

1 *The formal requirements of the publication,* such as the referencing system used, the number of copies required, the maximum number of words acceptable. Most journals inform authors of these in a printed section within each issue. Even so, it is surprising how many authors submit work that does not comply with requirements. Such authors start at a disadvantage in the publishing process. If in doubt, ask the publication for a list of its requirements, start off with an advantage, and save the time of having to rewrite. For example, if a journal states a maximum word length of 4000 words, don't submit an 8000-word paper. You may need to find another outlet for the longer work or recast the paper into two shorter ones with different focuses. This challenge of complying with formal requirements is within the grasp of all authors. A further challenge lies in adopting the appropriate writing style.

2 *The publisher's house style.* The preferred style of your chosen

publisher is worth researching, as you may have to adapt your written communication to comply with it. Alternatively, search for a publishing outlet whose preferred style matches your own natural writing style and submit your work to it.

3   *The content.* There is often a challenge involved in changing or adapting the *content* of your writing to suit the publisher's needs. It makes sense to find out what type of content different publishers and their readership require, before you start writing. These factors will influence what you include or exclude. For instance, a journal such as *Australian Social Work* looks for articles with a social work perspective and an Australian context. Some articles submitted may have intrinsic value but if they have no grounding in social work or do not relate in some way to the Australian context, they will probably need rewriting to include these elements. Oscar Wilde may have been able to say 'The play was a great success but the audience was a failure' (Ewart, 1984) when asked to comment on the reception of one of his least successful plays. Unfortunately, few authors can afford to ignore the audience if they wish to be successful—unless, of course, they enjoy Oscar Wilde's eminence.

In my experience, facing the above personal challenges at the outset lays the groundwork for successful writing for publication. The next set of challenges arises on completion of the written document and relates to the publication process itself.

Challenges in dealing with publishers

For me, dealing with publishers always contains three main challenges.

Finding the right outlet for your work
If you have researched your 'market' before writing anything, finding the right outlet for your work should be easier, as your communication will already be aimed at a particular audience and possibly a small known range of publications or outlets, and its style, content and context will reflect your research. As Jan Fook mentioned, *Author's Guide to Social Work Journals* (Mendelsohn, 1992) is a useful tool for social workers wishing to publish in journals, although of course it is not an exhaustive list for those selecting journal or book outlets. It is also helpful to know the current issues publishers may be favouring. For instance, one author told me recently that he had signed a contract for a 'non-secular' self-help book for people whose relationships have failed. 'The editor believes that "spiritual-

ity" is in,' said the author. Your entry into publishing will be easier if you too know what is 'in'.

If you are unsure which issues are popular, look out for journals or newsletters running calls for papers in particular areas. Submitting a paper on the topic in demand is often a good way for a new author to start on the publication trail.

If you can convince a publisher that a gap exists in the market for your type of book, you may also arouse interest that way. The same goes for in-house documents that are used for training and education. Starting with the least difficult forums and articles is obviously less daunting for a new author and is also a good way to 'test the water'. For example, presenting a seminar paper to a small group of colleagues may be the first step to a larger publishing project.

Just as successful advertising depends on sound market research, so does successful publishing. Having decided to send your communication to a particular publishing outlet, you face one of the greatest challenges of all—negotiating the reviewing process.

Negotiating the reviewing process

The publisher's decision to publish or not may depend on a myriad of factors. Some are negotiable, others are not.

In commercial publishing, the non-negotiable factors include the economic feasibility of a book or article. Publishers need to stay in business and make a profit, so they will judge a piece of writing according to whether there is a sufficient market for the product and a profit margin for the publisher. The idea may be an admirable one but it may founder through lack of a market.

Articles and books may also be rejected because too many submissions have been received in a particular area and the publisher has a limited need and/or budget for that area. They may be able to publish only one or two books in a specialist category each year or have one special edition of a journal on that topic. This brings to mind my own experience before having a children's book published. One editor said he liked the book but had already contracted another non-fiction children's book in the same category for that year and did not have the budget for another one. As Jan Fook observes, the rejection of a piece of work may not be a reflection on its intrinsic worth. If your work is rejected and you do not receive a written explanation, it does no harm to phone the editor and ask for feedback.

Given that there are no 'economic' obstacles to a publisher's accepting your article, how do you improve your chances of progressing through the selection process?

If you send your work to an outlet which has no formal independent refereeing process, the criteria upon which it is judged may be unstated. The decision to publish or not may be made solely by the editor or at a round table discussion of a selection panel. As such, it may be subject to their needs and biases at the time. Bear in mind, too, that some publishers exist to publish material with a particular bias, to support a particular stance, and it is useful to try and identify this from earlier publications. Once again, when in doubt I have usually found it informative to phone and speak to an editor about the selection process.

If you are submitting to a refereed journal, your article is likely to be reviewed according to a set of criteria. Most refereed journals have a system of blind review (the author's name is removed from the manuscript for review purposes) and at least two reviewers with expertise in the field are sought. In my own experience, where a piece of work is reviewed in light of set criteria by a referee who does not know the identity of the author, there is less chance of personal bias influencing the decision.

In the case of *Australian Social Work*, reviewers are expressly asked to return an article to the editor if they believe their values, theories or techniques preclude their reviewing a paper fairly. Of course, if reviewers' values closely match those of the author, the resultant review may have a favourable bias that is difficult to detect. Obtaining more than one review tends to offset this problem.

As mentioned, blind reviewing usually goes hand in hand with a set of defined criteria. Every article is measured against those guidelines. Reviewers for refereed social work journals are likely to assess articles according to some or all of the following characteristics, outlined below. Authors will improve their chances if they apply such a checklist to their own work.

Reviewers' checklist

- *Relevance and interest to readers*
This point relates to the need to write for a particular audience. For example, articles in social work journals need to be relevant and of interest to social workers!

- *Importance of the content to social workers*
Here reviewers will consider whether the article meets some of the following criteria:

a Is it timely? (and will it still be current in 12 months or more, when it is finally published?)
b Does it debate social issues?
c Does it anticipate future trends or reflect current ones?

---

d Does it reflect a fresh approach?
e Does it add depth to our existing knowledge?
f Does it relate to social work practice?
g Does it show evidence of original thinking or offer new insights in relation to social work practice or theory?
h Is it affirming for a social work audience?
i Does it challenge the reader to think or act differently?

It is important to bear in mind that some publishing outlets do specialise in *new* ideas and demand evidence of originality. Thus, even if an article, to quote Jan Fook, is 'expressed in such as way that an audience engages with it and finds it reaffirming and challenging', the article may not be acceptable for journals that specialise in new material. This again highlights the need to research your publication.

As an editor, I am also on the lookout for articles that report failures. If they include some critical analysis of the reason for failure, such articles are useful in helping others avoid similar pitfalls.

- *Argument and purpose of the article*
a Are they clear? It is important to outline the overall purpose of an article to let readers know why you decided to write it.
b Are they consistent?
c Are limits set on coverage, and is a clear focus established and maintained? In my experience this is often why research-based articles fail. The purpose is not clear or the articles try to cover too much. A research project may have covered many aspects and provided enough material for a book. To produce a small article you may need to focus in detail on only one or two aspects of the research.
d Given the stated limits, is the coverage adequate?
e Is there a logical order to the article?
f Is the argument sustained or does it digress from the main purpose?
g If the author is offering a critique, are alternative suggestions outlined?
h In a research article, is the methodology appropriate, clear and complete? Are the conclusions supported by the evidence; are implications for future research, policy and/or practice outlined; are results discussed in relation to previous research?

- *Appropriate documentation*
This may include:

a Description of experience
b Reference to previous publications
c Use of accepted social work models
d Analysis of data

For all types of documentation, reviewers will ask:

e Is it adequate?
f Is it accurate?

- *Organisation of material*

Jan Fook has already given a brief description of the headings normally used in writing up a research study. Detailed layouts are covered in various research texts and are well worth consulting before writing up research (see, for example, Babbie, 1990; Sarantakos, 1993).

Reviewers will look for the following organising details:

a Appropriate use of headings and sub-headings
b Use of clear charts, diagrams and tables that contain relevant information but do not confuse the reader
c Evidence the author has read and followed the guidelines for authors given by that publication
d Adequate, accurate and consistent refereeing
e Adequate linkages between ideas and sections to aid the flow of the article

- *Readability*

While ideas and content are the most important aspect of any article, ideas may founder if they are not reported in a readable fashion. Reviewers will therefore ask:

a Do the language and style detract from the content?
b Is the language clear and not too complex?
c Is there too much use of jargon
d Are technical terms adequately defined?
e Is the style appropriate to the publication?
f Some forums require all submissions to be written in the third person, some accept a mixture of the first and third person. Again, writers need to research their preferred forum.

The use of the first person can be refreshing and engaging if done well. However, to write well in the first person is *not* easy, particularly for the new writer. Too many 'I's' can be interpreted by the reader as self-promotion. You can still achieve a personal tone without the overuse of 'I', and this may be a safer option for first-time writers.

Once an article has been through the review process, the author usually receives a list of comments from the reviewers. These will vary in detail depending on the publication. Sometimes an article is accepted outright or rejected outright. More commonly, the author is asked to make changes to the article and is therefore faced with the final challenge: to revise/rewrite or not to revise/rewrite.

Revising and editing your work after it has been reviewed
If you receive critical feedback from reviewers and suggestions for change are given, you need to decide whether or not you are prepared to put in the effort required to incorporate these suggestions. If not, you may choose to submit the paper elsewhere, consider publishing it yourself (some publishers will publish your material if you cover the costs), or just file it away and put it down to good experience.

William Makepeace Thackeray chose the second option after writing his now classic novel *Vanity Fair*:

> He submitted it without success to every noted London publisher of the day, all of whom declined it. In desperation, he published it himself in monthly parts and only when it was a runaway success in this form did the publishers of the day exhibit any interest in it. (Hornadge, 1986, p.34)

Should you decide to proceed with the same publisher, I have found it useful to incorporate as many of the reviewers' recommendations as you think you can. If you disagree with some, explain why you did not incorporate them in a covering letter to the editor.

Jan Fook commented on the need to use your reviewers' feedback critically. This is a valid point, yet it is also my experience that some authors are never published *because they are too sensitive to, and not sufficiently open to, reviewers' criticisms.*

Perhaps Somerset Maugham was accurate when he said, in *Of Human Bondage*, 'People ask you for criticism but they only want praise' (1915). The tendency to reject criticisms outright is only human and yet, if you want to become a published author, you would do best to follow Jan Fook's suggestion to 'glean from [reviewers' feedback] that which you think to be important, relevant and helpful in improving your work'. It helps if you accept rewriting and editing—often many times—as part of the total writing process. At this stage it is comforting to remember that Ernest Hemingway rewrote parts of *A Farewell to Arms* up to 50 times!

Which brings us back to comparing the production of a play to the publication of a manuscript. Just as the script at the first rehearsal of a play is rarely the script that is heard on opening night, the author's first submission is rarely the text that is finally published.

If you wish to have your writing published, there are many challenges along the way to be faced and overcome.

REFERENCES

Babbie, E.R. (1990) *Survey Research Methods*, Wadsworth, Belmont, California

Browne, E. (1990) 'Social workers as writers: The process of writing—A personal account', *Australian Social Work*, vol. 43, no. 1, p.1

Ewart, N. (1984) *The Writer and the Reader*, Blandford Press, Dorset

French, S. (1993) 'Telling', in Shakespeare, P., Atkinson, D. and French, S. (eds) *Reflecting on Research Practice*, Open University Press, Buckingham

Hornadge, B. (1986) *How to Publish Your Own Book: A Complete Guide to Self-publishing in Australia*, Review Publications, Dubbo

Maugham, W.S. (1915) *Of Human Bondage*, Heinemann, London

Mendelsohn, H. (1992) *The Author's Guide to Social Work Journals*, 3rd edn, NASW, Washington DC

Mills, C. W. (1970) *The Sociological Imagination*, Penguin, Harmondsworth

Pope, A. (1709) 'An essay on criticism', in Dobree, B. (ed.) (1956) *Alexander Pope's Collected Poems*, J.M. Dent & Sons, London

Rabbitts, E.G. (1990) 'Practitioners as writers', *Australian Social Work*, vol.43, no. 4, p.2

Sarantakos, S. (1993) *Social Research*, Macmillan Education Australia, Melbourne

Schilling, R., Schink, S. and Gilchrist, L. (1985) 'Utilization of social work research: Reaching the practitioner', *Social Work*, vol. 29, Nov.–Dec. pp.527–529

Sheafor, B. *et al.* (1988) *Techniques and Guidelines for Social Work Practice*, Allyn & Bacon, Newton

Williams, L. and Hopps, G. (1987) 'Publication as a practice goal: Enhancing opportunities for social workers', *Social Work*, vol. 32, Sept–Oct. pp.373–376

Part VI
Making connections

15 Making connections: Reflective practices and formal theories
Jan Fook

At the beginning of this book I described how I came to develop a reflective approach through my own research, teaching and practice experience. All the contributors have in turn recounted aspects of their research practice experience and the ways in which their formulations about research theory changed through the process. Although I was fascinated by the unique formulation of each contributor's experience, I was equally intrigued by the unintentional similarities in their accounts. In this closing chapter I will try to identify some of the themes that have arisen from these accounts, and will end by connecting some of the issues raised in the book with some more formalised theories that may help readers to take and further develop these ideas in their own practice and thinking.

SOME MAJOR THEMES

The challenge of implicit assumptions

Sue Gleed's honest account of her doubts about her ability to undertake research is a pertinent example of the ways in which our implicit assumptions can undermine our effectiveness. Sue began to realise that her early attitude to social work research (that it was somehow separate from practice) was not helpful in enabling her to actually carry out a research project. Recognising the similarities between practice and research was helpful.

Similarly, Denise Sadique recognised that her assumptions that

189

her research should be comprehensive and unassailable put unnecessary pressure on her to achieve goals which, although admirable, were probably unattainable. She risked jeopardising the quality of her work because of these assumptions. Martin Ryan found that his implicit 'quantitative' assumptions made it difficult for him to undertake the transition to qualitative work, and that only by challenging his ideas about the value of 'subjective' interpretations was he able to move on.

Carmel Laragy's experience was a little different. She started from an explicitly espoused positivist approach to research but, interestingly, found that other explicit action-oriented assumptions she held in relation to other aspects of her social work practice were actually more congruent with a more participative action approach. It then simply became a matter of using an explicit framework that was more congruent with her practice.

Unintended outcomes and the unattainability of control

Helen Cleak spoke of outcomes from her and her colleagues' research which, although unforeseen, were often positive (and often not so positive). This theme, of research's having unanticipated results either in the formalised findings of the study or through the process and experience of the research, is echoed by many of the contributors. Our researchers were often bewildered, frustrated, delighted or annoyed because participants and research contexts refused to behave in ways conducive to the smooth implementation of the projects.

Ann Ingamells found that although her philosophy was to encourage full participation and collaboration, her research colleagues wanted her to take the leadership in pulling ideas together. Sometimes study participants do not share our research philosophy, and we are forced to modify our ideals accordingly. Sometimes we must modify our ideals for other reasons. Although Marg Lynn held a philosophy of collaborative research, she chose (with regret) to limit her idealised approach for a purely pragmatic reason—lack of time.

Gary Hough's and Bill Healy's experiences were slightly different again. Both found that even though some of their research participants might have been willing, the politics of their situations, particularly community and governmental events, very much determined how and when the research took place as well as the type of findings attained. In Bob Doyle's case, his primarily research-oriented project evolved to become an instrument of organisational change. The researcher's lack of control is clearly part and parcel of the situation and as such perhaps needs to be accepted and worked with as part of the research process, rather than being seen as a problem to be mastered. Our personal pre-determined research philosophies and intentions, while unable to be perfectly secured during the research process, may nevertheless become enriched through the vagaries of the research experience. Linette Hawkins's account of her struggle in undertaking her research project, which she embarked upon while being firmly committed to a different type of approach, is a moving illustration of this type of development.

My own experience of undertaking theoretical development research on radical casework in some ways underscores the theme of the struggle for 'ideological purity' in conducting research. My research was explicitly designed on structured positivist lines, but I unexpectedly found the experience empowering, and I understand many readers of the work have found it enabling. Despite our pure theoretical intentions, other people may experience and interpret our work in quite different terms which are often, indeed usually, outside our control.

SOME MAJOR THEORIES

What are some of the more formalised theoretical traditions which relate to the themes raised by this book and the contributors' experiences? In what follows I will try to recount, briefly and succinctly, some of the major areas of literature, debate and research which help to develop these themes, so that readers might explore some of this thinking a little further. Many of the relevant theoretical formulations express themselves in different ways, some as longstanding debates, some as particular movements within specific disciplines (such as education), and others in terms of more formal ideological or theoretical approaches. In that sense they overlap and interrelate rather than existing as discrete ideological formulations. I have attempted to identify what I believe to be some of the major relevant influences, and will describe them in no particular order except as they might appear familiar to the reader.

The critique of technique

Some of the earliest calls to a more reflective style of social work came from criticisms of 'technicist' approaches to social work, which place prime importance on developing techniques and technologies to improve social work practice. Critics of this view argue that some of the implicit values of the 'technological fix' actually subvert the social justice and caring values of social work and are implicitly conservative, in that a mere change of technique diverts attention from structural change (Saleebey, 1991). Earlier radical social work critics also touted this view (Fook, 1993, p.9). The laboratory-style teaching of micro skills, free from value or contextual considerations, has also been criticised from a feminist perspective (Fook, 1988; 1989) and for its disempowering effect (Rossiter, 1993).

Criticisms of technique-oriented approaches are often aligned with criticisms of the use of positivist paradigms in social work, which assume that the way forward for social work lies in the development of 'scientific' methods based on empirically verifiable and generalisable theories. In this type of view, 'objective, value free knowledge is considered to be the ultimate' (Harre Hindmarsh, 1992, p.24), and on the basis of this professional body of knowledge, techniques are devised through the application of linear (cause to effect) reasoning. Thus rationality, as a way of knowing and controlling our world, is also valued.

There are many critics of a purely positivist approach. They argue that technical approaches and related scientific approaches to knowledge are incongruent with the types of situations with which social workers must deal and the kinds of ways in which they work (Gowdy, 1994; Kondrat, 1992). This type of argument of course underlies the well-regarded work of Argyris and Schon (1974) and Schon (1983; 1987), who have applied their work across several different professions. Their simple challenge to 'technical rationality', and their development of an alternative conceptualisation of theory and practice, strike a chord with many social workers (Papell & Skolnik, 1992) and is one body of work that has motivated the writing of this book.

Other works by non-social workers are relevant, particularly the work of Dreyfus and Dreyfus (1986) in studying the development of professional expertise in decision making in complex situations. They formulated a five-stage theory of professional development, beginning with the novice's reliance on formalised rules constructed out of context, through a process of development of situationally based rules from experience, to a stage in which actions are largely intuitive and based on a long history of recognition of complex patterns. Originally constructed as a challenge to the artificial intelligence movement, their work implicitly challenges purely technicist approaches, in that their study revealed the extent to which expert practice is intuitive and therefore often inaccessible to purely technical analysis, description and duplication.

The unity of theory, practice and research

Related to the criticism of scientific and technical approaches to social work has been the argument that such paradigms have been responsible for the artificial dichotomies between 'theory' and 'practice', and 'research' and 'practice' (Harre Hindmarsh, 1992).

The argument for the integration of theory and practice is an old one, and is familiar to every social worker. In the 1960s and 1970s Marxists spoke about the need for the linking of theory and action in 'praxis', and in the 1970s and 1980s, Freireans and feminists stressed the development of critical consciousness and the linking of action and awareness (Fook, 1993).

More recently the argument has turned to the development of alternative paradigms, which allow us to reconceptualise the relationships between theory, practice and research. Some researchers have couched the debate in research methodological terms and argued for the importance of qualitative approaches to research (Reissman, 1994). Others have highlighted the interpretive nature of social work practice and research and called for congruent methods and approaches (Heineman Pieper, 1990; Scott, 1989; 1990, Rodwell, 1987). In some areas the debate has become passionate, and has seen the opposing sides become polarised: 'My paradigm can beat your paradigm' (Haworth, 1991). For some years the debate has been reflected in our tendency to become almost frozen into asking questions like whether social work is a science or an art (Goldstein, 1990; Siporin, 1988), but perhaps the way ahead lies in formulating paradigms which avoid these simple dichotomies.

Peile is one of the more recent writers who attempt to develop an approach to social work that unites practice, theory and research (1988a; 1988b; 1993; 1994a). He is, as might be expected, critical of positivistic approaches, but he also criticises 'post-positivism' in that, while it is open to multiple methods, it does not recognise the participation of research subjects, or that we are constantly engaged, implicitly, in a process of theorising, research and practice (1994b, p.20). His 'reformulated positivism' would incorporate, among a plethora of action, reflective and experiential approaches (1994b, p.22) the participatory action research and related new paradigm approaches (see for example, Reason, 1988; Carr & Kemmis, 1986; Wadsworth, 1984; Whyte, 1991).

Reflectivity and related techniques and processes

The importance of reflective process in the development of practice and theory was the point at which we began this book and is an approach whose development has run alongside that of the other themes discussed in this section. As mentioned earlier, Argyris and Schon (1976) and Schon (1983; 1987) are principal exponents of the view. In brief, they note that there is often a yawning gap between the formalised theory which professionals believe themselves to be enacting ('espoused theory'), and that which is implicit in their practice ('theory in use'). They advocate reflective teaching approaches which allow professionals to uncover the theory implicit in their practice in order to redevelop their practice more in line with their desired theory. This was referred to as a process of developing a 'theory of action'.

The reflective process they advocate shares some similarities with other research methods, in particular the critical incident technique, which was first developed by Flanagan (1954). This technique, of asking research subjects to describe a specific incident that was critical (significant) to them, provides a useful way of gaining concrete and in-depth information about specific happenings which are then able to be researched in multiple ways. The simple act of asking a person to describe an incident that was critical to them elicits valuable concrete information about how that person experiences their world. It is particularly useful for researching areas which are not easily accessible to another party. Critical incident technique is useful in social work practice (Davis & Reid,1988) and in teaching (Brookfield, 1986; Fook et al., 1994; Cooper, 1994). It has been used successfully in the research of professional practice across a variety of fields (for example, Benner, 1984) and has been advocated as a method for studying professional competencies (Gonczi et al.,1990).

Interestingly enough, critical incident technique is not dissimilar to some of the narrative techniques which have arisen more recently, to some degree out of postmodern approaches (which I will discuss in some detail a little further on). For instance in family therapy, narrative techniques analyse and seek to change the ways in which families' myths or stories maintain unwanted dynamics (White & Epston, 1989; Hartman, 1991). Narrative analysis is, of course, also used as a research technique and is related to semiotic analysis (Kellehear, 1993, pp.42–50) in that the narrator's use of language is interpreted or *deconstructed* to reveal hidden meanings. I will discuss the relationship of these types of techniques to postmodernism and post-structuralism a little further on.

Experiential approaches, adult education, and problem-based learning

In some ways a reflective approach also implies the importance of experiential learning (Moffat, 1994) in that the learner learns best through reflection on actual and immediate experience. Both the adult education movement (Knowles, 1978; Coulshed, 1993) and the problem-based learning approach incorporate reflective and experiential elements.

In brief, the adult learning approach is based on a number of premises—that the adult learner moves towards a self-concept of autonomy; uses life experiences as resources for learning; and is more likely to learn when learning is directed towards dealing with present (rather than future) life situations, rather than towards acquiring knowledge for its own sake, and when it is focused on what the student wants to learn rather than what the teacher wants to teach (Knowles, 1978; The Field Education Manual Project Group, 1991). When these points are summarised as principles of autonomy, situational immediacy and relevance, it can be seen that the adult learning approach shares assumptions with the earlier discussed critiques of technicism, and reflective approaches.

The problem-solving or problem-based learning approach (Vinson *et al.*, 1986; Burgess, 1992) picks up on some of these themes and develops them into a particular approach to curriculum design. Learning is organised in small groups around encountering particular 'problems' rather than being taught in traditional lectures in subject or discipline areas. The approach is based on some similar adult learning assumptions—that students learn best when actually engaged in (or experiencing) solving a problem and when able to use previous experience and have some responsibility for their own learning. Additionally, the approach assumes that better learning occurs when theoretical and practical learning can be integrated, and that the process of collaborative learning is also important (Burgess, 1992, p.2).

Feminist perspectives

Feminist theorists have challenged traditional approaches to ways of knowing and the implications for teaching and learning (Belenky *et al.*, 1986; Dore, 1994), practice and research (Swigonowski, 1994; Stanley & Wise, 1990). In their landmark work, Belenky and her colleagues (1986), in interviews with 135 women, formulated a theory of womens' knowledge acquisition in which they must progress from an initial stage of 'silence', in which they experience themselves as voiceless and mindless in the face of external educative authorities. On the basis of this research the authors were able to identify particular barriers to women's learning and to posit more 'connected' ways of teaching and learning. According to Dore (1994, p.100) the overarching goals of feminist pedagogy are: 'the empowerment of all participants in the learning process, students as well as teacher; the development of a sense of community in which all share equally in the learning task; and the realisation of the capacity for leadership as an outgrowth of taking responsibility for one's own learning and the learning of others'.

The feminist standpoint on research criticises positivist approaches in relation to three areas:

- the assumption of the possibiltiy of value-free scientific activity;
- the separation of subject and object; and
- the belief in an objective reality (Swigonowski, 1994, pp.388–389).

It is therefore important to recognise the importance of subjectivity in all aspects of research and practice. This is often termed 'reflexivity' (Stevens, 1993), and feminists emphasise the need to reflect continually on the ways in which the researcher influences the situation. This might involve recognising the ways in which the researcher's own individual awareness affects the situation, particularly through particular interpretations or constructions of meaning in different situations. Stanley (1990) provides a useful list of sites at which it is important to recognise and reaffirm a feminist perspective:

- the relationship between the researcher/s and the researched group
- the recognition of emotion as a research experience
- the intellectual autobiography of the researcher/s
- the management of the different 'realities' or perspectives or meanings of the researcher/s and the researched group
- the question of power in research and writing.

Postmodernism and post-structuralism

Many of the foregoing ideas have been developed through postmodern and post-structuralist theory, which is beginning to be recognised as a legitimate and valuable perspective in social work (Featherstone & Fawcett, 1994; Leonard, 1994; Solas, 1994; Healy & Fook, in press). I do not want to get too involved in detailed argument about the difference between postmodernism and post-structuralism, but for the purposes of the discussion here, I believe postmodernism to be indicative of a current perspective for theorising cultural conditions across a number of disciplines (the arts, humanities, sciences and professions), whereas I take post-structuralism to emerge more from the tradition of social theory.

Postmodernism in its simplest sense is an analysis of global conditions based on the idea that we have moved on from a modernist age in which we sought to 'establish reliable foundations for generalisable knowledge, policy and practice' (Parton, 1994, p.28). Postmodernism recognises that attempts to unify and control our world through organised knowledge and meaning frameworks ('grand narratives' of Science, Reason, Enlightenment, Humanism) and structured hierarchies (the nation state, government) have become fragmented. As Turner phrases it (1992, p.142) 'we live in a constructed metaphorical reality'. In this sense, the metaphors, or 'narratives' or 'discourses' become important in understanding the ways in which we make meaning of our world ('construct our realities'). Post-structuralists therefore place great importance on the language we use and how it frames our ways of knowing the world.

The term post-structuralism is generally taken to refer to the work of the French social theorists Foucault, Derrida and Lacan. They challenged 'structuralists' (like Marx, Freud) who tended to believe that the meaning of superficial phenomena could be explained by underlying organising structures, and was therefore fixed. Post-structuralists, however, argue that meaning is open to multiple interpretations, and changes in relation to context (Weedon, 1987).

Sands and Nuccio (1992) very usefully summarise the main themes of post-structuralism:

- criticism of logocentrism (the belief that there is a fixed, singular or logical order);
- the recognition of differences and the resistance to binary-oppositional thinking. A logocentric view often implies binary categorisation of phenomena into mutually exclusive and oppositional hierarchies (e.g. male–female). Usually one part of the binary is valued (privileged) over the other. We need to recognise that there is a wealth of meaning which does not fit into these categories;
- deconstruction. It is important to *deconstruct* our discourses (language) in order to resist logocentrism (decentre) and to discover mutliple, contextual and devalued meanings;
- recognition of the existence of multiple discourses;
- subjectivity (the social construction of one's identity) is contextually influenced and is therefore 'situated', which means that it may be changing, contradictory and multifaceted.

In addition, the work of Foucault provides a useful conceptualisation of *power* through its relationship to language and institutional practices. Since knowledge is controlled through discourses, the exercise of power is therefore about the ways in which some discourses become dominant over others.

POSSIBILITIES FOR REFLECTIVE PRACTICE

By way of summary, reflective practice questions purely rational ways of knowing the world and rebalances them with subjective, intuitive and inductive approaches, thus lending support to new paradigms which integrate theorising, practice and research as part of holistic experience. Experiential approaches to learning, which value the autonomy and participation of the learner, share similar assumptions, as do feminist perspectives, which also emphasise connected ways of knowing, the recognition of the personal and subjective, and the ways in which power relations influence practice.

At face value, post-structuralism appears potentially destructive. However, I prefer to see it as a framework that allows us to revalue the approaches discussed in this chapter, many of which also happen to be long-standing tenets of social work practice wisdom. First, for example, a fundamental principle is that social workers deal with the context of the 'person in situation'. Post-structuralist perspectives add complex dimensions to this concept by emphasising the import-ance not only of context but of multiple and changing contexts in interpreting situations, influencing subjectivity, and affecting power relations.

Second, social workers have long been aware of the importance of emotional and subjective (in addition to primarily rational) aspects of human experience. Post-structuralist theory, with its questioning of the value of purely rational and logical ways of understanding the world (and its critique of the scientific paradigm), lends theoretical credibility to alternative ways of knowing.

Third, social workers have long been in the business of 'deconstructing'—trying to determine meanings or agendas which might not be immediately evident in the 'presenting problem'. How-ever, adopting the deconstructive stance of post-structuralism and turning a critical, deconstructive gaze on ourselves has a potentially liberating effect. Once we recognise that our world as we know and understand it is constructed by the frameworks (discourses) *we ourselves* have devised for knowing and understanding it, we can begin to change it by changing the ways in which we have con-structed, and continue to construct it.

> Our world is continually offered as one of ready made customs, traditions and order-to-the-things of daily life. Yet the natural order is not natural or inevitable, but constructed historically, socially and with political interest . . .
>
> To make our social situation problematic, not as an order of things but as outcomes of the collective actions of men and women, is to make these situations potentially alterable and amenable to human agency. (Popkewitz, as quoted in Harre Hindmarsh, 1992, p.12)

If we also accept that discourses and related constructions often exist and are maintained by particular power relations in particular and changing contexts, a deconstructive analysis can indicate ways in which existing power relations might be challenged.

Post-structuralist theory, then, not only supports reflective approaches to practice but also holds the critical potential to free us from fixed and potentially restrictive ways of thinking, and may indicate avenues for change. This analysis in particular applies to the ways we have constructed our notions of theory, practice and research. Harre Hindmarsh (1992) analyses social work by arguing that our current formulations of theory, practice and research rest on an essentially positivist paradigm: divisions have been constructed between the worlds of theory, practice and research which have tended to privilege theory/research over practice. Why have we framed the different worlds in this way, and why do we seek to perpetuate these divisions? What sorts of power relations uphold or are assumed by these distinctions? Who wants to keep it this way and why? Why do some of us cling to a positivist paradigm? Should we seek to formulate ways of knowing and understanding our world which are more in line with social work as we have otherwise conceptualised it—as a contextual, holistic, complex, unpredictable and changing practice informed by multiple and marginal perspectives? Somehow, simple divisions between theory, practice and research do not sit easily with this picture. Perhaps a reflective approach to our experience may integrate these worlds in ways that are more congruent with that uncertain entity we know as social work.

REFERENCES

Argyris, C. and Schon, D. (1974) *Theory in Practice: Increasing Professional Effectiveness*, Jossey-Bass, San Francisco

Belenky, M., Clinchy, B., Goldberger, N. and Tarule, J. (1986) *Women's Ways of Knowing*, Basic Books, New York

Benner, P. (1984) *From Novice to Expert*, Addison-Wesley, Menlo Park

Brookfield, S. D. (1987) *Developing Critical Thinkers*, Open University Press, Milton Keynes

Burgess, H. (1992) *Problem-Led Learning for Social Work*, Whiting & Birch, London

Carr, W. and Kemmis, S. (1986) *Becoming Critical*, Deakin University Press, Geelong

Cooper, L. (1994) 'Critical story telling in social work education', *Australian Journal of Adult and Community Education*, vol. 34, no. 2, pp.131–141

Coulshed, V. (1993) 'Adult learning: Implications for teaching in social work education', *British Journal of Social Work*, vol. 23, pp.1–13

Davis, I.P. and Reid, W.J. (1988) 'Event analysis in clinical practice and research', *Social Casework*, May, pp.298–306

Dore, M.M. (1994) 'Feminist pedagogy and the teaching of social work practice', *Journal of Social Work Education*, vol. 30, no.1, Winter, pp.97–106

Dreyfus, H. and Dreyfus, S. (1986) *Mind Over Machine*, Free Press, New York

Featherstone, B. and Fawcett, B. (1994) 'Oh no! Not more isms: Feminism, postmodernism and post-structuralism and social work education', Paper delivered at the 27th Congress of the International Association of Schools of Social Work, Amsterdam, July

Flanagan, J. (1954) 'The critical incident technique', *Psychological Bulletin*, vol. 51, no. 4, pp.327–358

Fook, J. (1988) 'Teaching casework: Incorporating radical and feminist perspectives into the current curriculum', in Berren, R., Grace, D., James, D. and Vinson, T. (eds) *Advances in Social Welfare Education*, Heads of Schools of Social Work in Australia, UNSW, pp.43–53

——(1989) 'Teaching casework: Incorporating radical and feminist perspectives into the current curriculum Part II', in Berren, R., Grace, D., James, D. and Vinson, T. (eds) *Advances in Social Welfare Education*, Heads of Schools of Social Work in Australia, UNSW, pp.93–105

Fook, J., Ryan, M. and Hawkins, L. (1994) 'Becoming a social worker: Educational implications from preliminary findings of a longitudinal study', *Social Work Education*, vol. 13, no. 2, pp.5–26

Goldstein, H. (1990) 'The knowledge base of social work practice: Theory, wisdom, analogue, or art?' *Families in Society*, January, pp.32–43

Gonczi, A., Hager, P. and Oliver, L. (1990) *Establishing Competency Based Standards in the Professions*, Australian Government Publishing Service, Canberra

Gowdy, E. (1994) 'From technical rationality to participating consciousness', *Social Work*, vol. 39, no. 4, July, pp.362–370

Harre Hindmarsh, J. (1992) *Social Work Oppositions*, Avebury, Aldershot

Hartman, A. (1991) 'Words create worlds', *Social Work*, vol. 36, no. 4, pp.275–276

Haworth, G. (1991) 'My paradigm can beat your paradigm: Some reflections on knowledge conflicts', *Sociology and Social Welfare*, vol. 18, no. 4, December, pp.35–50

Healy, B. and Fook, J. (in press) 'Re-inventing social work', *Advances in Social Work Education*

Heineman Pieper, M. (1990) 'The heuristic paradigm: A unifying and comprehensive approach to social work research', *Smith College Studies in Social Work*, vol. 60, no. 1, pp.8–34

Kellehear, A. (1993) *The Unobtrusive Researcher*, Allen & Unwin, Sydney

Knowles, M. (1978) *The Adult Learner; A Neglected Species*, Gulf Publishing, London

Kondrat, M. (1992) 'Reclaiming the practical: Formal and substantive rationality in social work practice', *Social Service Review*, vol. 66, no. 2, June, pp.237–255

Lather, P. (1991) *Feminist Research in Education: Within/Against*, Deakin University Press, Geelong

Leonard, P. (1994) 'Knowledge/power and postmodernism: Implications for the practice of a critical social work education', *Canadian Social Work Review*, vol. 11, no. 1, Winter, pp.11–26

Moffat, K. (1994) 'Teaching social work practice as a reflective process', Paper delivered at the 27th Congress of the International Association of Schools of Social Work, Amsterdam, July

Papell, C.P. and Skolnik, L. (1992) 'The reflective practitioner: A contemporary paradigm's relevance for social work education', *Journal of Social Work Education*, vol. 28, no. 1, pp.18–26

Parton, N. (1994) 'Problematics of government: (Post)modernity and social work', *British Journal of Social Work*, vol. 24, pp.9–32

Peile, C. (1988a) 'Research paradigms in social work: From stalemate to creative synthesis', *Social Service Review*, vol. 62, no. 1, pp.1–19

——(1988b) 'The unity of research and practice: Creative practitioner research for social work', in Chamberlain, E. (ed.) *Change and Continuity in Australian Social Work*, Longman Cheshire, Melbourne, pp.69–83

——(1994a) *The Creative Paradigm: Insight, Synthesis and Knowledge Development*, Avebury, Aldershot

——(1994b) 'Theory, practice and research: Casual acquaintances or a seamless whole?', *Australian Social Work*, June, vol. 47, no. 2, pp.18–23

Reason, P. (1988) *Human Inquiry in Action*, Sage, London

Reissman, C. (1994) *Qualitative Studies in Social Work Research*, Sage, Thousand Oaks

Rodwell, M. K. (1987) 'Naturalistic inquiry: An alternative model for social work assessment', *Social Service Review*, June, pp.231–246

Rossiter, A. (1993) 'Teaching from a critical perspective: Towards empowerment in social work education', *Canadian Social Service Review*, vol. 10, no. 1, Winter, pp.76–90

Saleebey, D. (1991) 'Technological fix: Altering the consciousness of the social work profession', *Sociology and Social Welfare*, vol. 18, no. 4, December, pp.51–76

Sands, R. and Nuccio, K. (1992) 'Postmodern feminist theory and social work', *Social Work*, vol. 37, no. 6, November, pp.480–494

Schon, D. (1983) *The Reflective Practitioner*, Basic Books, New York

——(1987) *Educating the Reflective Practitioner*, Jossey-Bass, San Francisco

Scott, D. (1989) 'Meaning construction and social work practice', *Social Service Review*, March, pp.39–51

——(1990) 'Practice wisdom: The neglected source of practice research', *Social Work*, vol. 35, no. 6, November, pp.564–568

Siporin, M. (1988) 'Clinical social work as art form', *Social Casework*, vol. 69, no. 3, pp.177–183

Solas, J. (1994) *(De)Constructing Social Work Education*, Avebury, Aldershot

Stanley, L. and Wise, S. (1990) 'Method, methodology and epistemology', in Stanley, L. (ed.) (1990) *Feminist Praxis: Research, Theory and Epistemology in Feminist Sociology*, Routledge, London, pp.20–60

Stevens, L. (1993) 'Reflexivity: Recognising subjectivity in research', in Colquhoun, D. and Kellehear, A. *Health Research in Practice*, Chapman & Hall, London, pp.152–170

Swigonowski, M. E. (1994) 'The logic of feminist standpoint theory for social work research', *Social Work*, vol. 39, no. 4, July, pp.387–393

The Field Education Manual Project Group (1991) *A Handbook for Field Educators*, Australian Association of Social Work and Welfare Education, Charles Sturt University, Wagga Wagga

Turner, B.S. (1992) *Regulating Bodies*, Basic Books, New York

Vinson, T., Leu, L., Smith, B. & Yamey, N. (1986) 'A problem-solving approach to social work education', *Australian Social Work*, vol. 39, no. 3, pp.3–8

Wadsworth, Y. (1984) *Do It Yourself Social Research*, Victorian Council of Social Service, Collingwood, Victoria

Weedon, C. (1987) *Feminist Practice and Poststructuralist Theory*, Basil Blackwell, London

White, M. and Epston, D. (1989) *Literate Means to Therapeutic Ends*, Dulwich Centre Publications, Adelaide

Whyte, W. F. (ed.) (1991) *Participatory Action Research*, Sage, Newbury

Index